Reading Comprehension

Nonfiction

Grade **3**

Writing: Barbara Allman
Editorial Development: Teera Safi
Kira Freed
Lisa Vitarisi Mathews
Copy Editing: Anna Pelligra
Art Direction: Cheryl Puckett
Art Coordination: Kathy Kopp
Cover Design: Yuki Meyer
Illustration: Greg Harris
Design/Production: Marcia Smith
Jessica Onken

EMC 3263
Visit
teaching-standards.com
to view a correlation
of this book.

**Correlated to
Current Standards**

CPSIA: Sheridan Saline, Inc., Saline, MI, USA [10/2023]

Contents

Introduction

Units

Science Articles

Social Studies Articles

Geography Article

Biography Articles

Technology Article

What's in Every Unit?

Teacher resource pages are provided for lesson preparation and instructional guidance.

The Guided Reading Level helps identify appropriate texts.

Student objectives and content-area concepts are indicated.

A suggested learning path helps you pace the lesson.

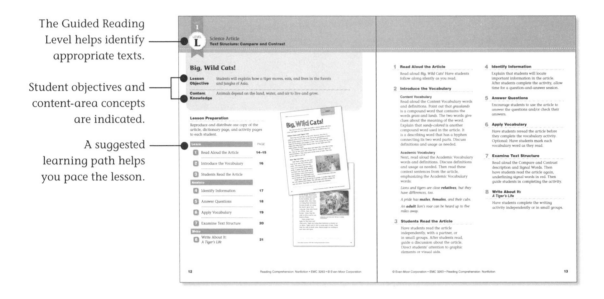

Content-area articles with embedded nonfiction text structures provide a variety of reading experiences.

Nonfiction Text Structures include:
- Question and Answer
- Cause and Effect
- Main Idea and Details
- Compare and Contrast
- Time Order

Labels indicate the content area.

Art and graphics provide additional information and context.

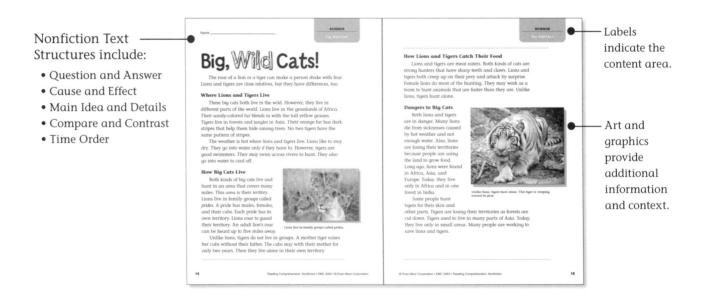

Student pages provide support for understanding the vocabulary, concepts, and structure of the text.

Dictionary

A dictionary page defines content and academic vocabulary words to help students better understand their use in the article.

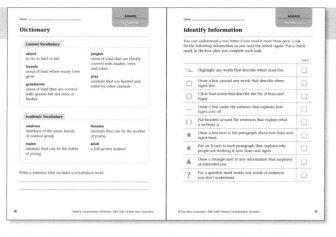

Identify Information

A close reading activity guides students to interact with the text and identify important information.

Answer Questions

A reading comprehension activity asks students to answer questions about the article, prompting them to examine it closely, and provides an informal assessment of students' understanding.

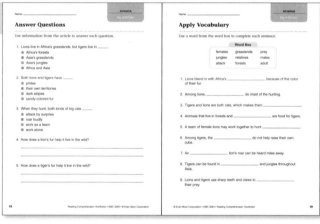

Apply Vocabulary

A vocabulary activity provides students another opportunity to interact with key words from the article and apply them in a different context.

Text Structure

A text structure activity asks students to examine how information in the article is organized.

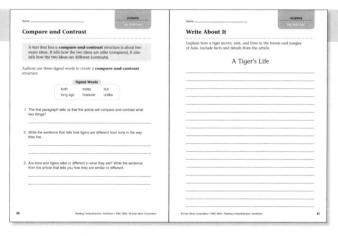

Write About It

The unit culminates with a text-based writing assignment.

Five Elements

A reproducible chart examines the five elements of informational texts, explains what each element is, and offers guiding questions to improve students' understanding of texts.

Five Structures

A reproducible chart describes how informational texts are organized and points out signal words associated with each text structure.

Vocabulary Definitions

account: a record of the money that a person keeps in a bank

adobe: mud and straw bricks that are baked in the sun

adult: a full-grown animal

allegiance: respect for someone or something

ancient: from a time long ago

angle: a side or a view of something

archaeologists: scientists who study people of long ago by digging up pots, tools, and other things left behind

attack: to try to hurt or kill

attend: to go to

average: usual; most common

bromeliad: a rainforest plant that can live off water in the air instead of water in the soil

business: a place where people work to make money and where customers spend money

cafes: coffeehouses; restaurants that serve coffee

canals: waterways dug across land for ships to go through

check: a written order telling a bank to pay an amount from a person's checking account

citizens: people who, by law, belong to a country

clasp: a small hook that holds parts together

climate: the weather patterns in an area

coast: seashore; land next to the sea

code: a set of rules to be followed

connected: joined together

Continental Congress: the main government of the United States when it was becoming a country

court: a group of judges who meet to decide cases of the law; the place where cases of the law are decided

debit card: a small plastic card used to buy things; the money comes out of a checking account

degrees (°): units of measure for temperature

deposit: to put money into an account

description: words that tell about something

display: to put something in a place where people can see it

Reading Comprehension: Nonfiction • EMC 3263 • © Evan-Moor Corporation

Vocabulary Definitions, *continued*

dwellings: places where people live

edit: to be in charge of a magazine or other project; to decide what gets printed in a magazine

elected: chosen by a vote to do a job

enslaved: forced to work for others without pay

equal rights: freedoms that all people should have

Fahrenheit: a system for measuring temperature in which water freezes at 32° and boils at 212°

fasten: to join two things together

females: animals that can be the mother of young

forests: areas of land where many trees grow

gatherings: meetings

glaciers: very large pieces of ice

grasslands: areas of land that are covered with grasses but not trees or bushes

hire: to give a job to

honor: a show of respect

ice ages: times long ago when ice covered the world

ideals: ideas about what would be perfect or best

improve: to make better

invented: created something new

iron: a valuable type of metal

jungles: areas of land that are thickly covered with bushes, trees, and vines

justice: a judge; a person who decides cases in a court of law

law school: a school where people study laws

lawyer: a person who knows the laws and helps people in court

layers: something on or between other things

loans: money that is lent to people to use for a period of time

males: animals that can be the father of young

materials: things used to make other things

medicines: things that are used to treat or cure sickness

mystery: something that is hidden or unknown

orchids: plants with bright flowers that have odd shapes

patent: a piece of paper showing that you own an invention

Vocabulary Definitions, *continued*

pay: money you get for doing a job

pledge: to promise; a promise

prey: animals that are hunted and eaten by other animals

proper: correct

protect: to keep safe

pueblo: a Native American village built from stone and adobe

rainforest: a thick forest in an area that is often hot and rainy

region: a certain place, space, or area

relatives: members of the same family or animal group

saddle: a seat for a rider on a horse

salute: to show a sign of respect with a special hand motion

scientists: people who study science

shave ice: a Hawaiian treat made with shaved ice and fruit flavors

soak: to take in a liquid, such as through roots

spears: tools used for hunting that have sharp points and long, straight handles

spices: flavorings for food that are made from plant parts

stepfather: a man who marries a child's mother and is not the child's birth father

surf: large waves that roll onto the seashore

symbol: a thing that stands for something else

temperature: a measure of the amount of heat in something

temples: buildings where some people go to practice their religion

treasures: things that are special or that have value

tropical: having to do with a hot, wet part of Earth

united: joined together

unusual: not common or ordinary

valuable: having worth or value

waterway: a body of water that ships can travel through

windmill: a tall machine with blades that spin in the wind to pump water

withdraw: to take money out of an account

Reading Comprehension: Nonfiction • EMC 3263 • © Evan-Moor Corporation

Overview of Articles and Writing Prompts

Title	Level	Content Area	Text Structure	Writing Prompt
Big, Wild Cats!	L	Life Science	Compare and Contrast	Informative/ Explanatory
Sandra Day O'Connor	L	Biography (Political Science)	Time Order	Informative/ Explanatory
Barack Obama	M	Biography (Political Science)	Time Order	Informative/ Explanatory
Plants of the Rainforest	N	Life Science	Main Idea and Details (Enumeration)	Argument
The Great Lakes	N	Geography	Cause and Effect	Informative/ Explanatory
Two Climates	O	Earth Science	Compare and Contrast	Opinion
It's a Grand Old Flag	O	Social Studies (Sociology)	Main Idea and Details (Enumeration)	Informative/ Explanatory
The Mystery of Mesa Verde	O	Social Studies (U.S. History)	Time Order	Informative/ Explanatory
About Banks	P	Social Studies (Economics)	Question and Answer	Argument
The Zipper	P	Social Studies (Sociology)	Cause and Effect	Informative/ Explanatory

Name: _____

Five Elements of Nonfiction Text

An **element** is something you can think about or look for in nonfiction texts.

- Seeing elements in a text helps you understand what it is about.
- Most nonfiction texts have the elements listed in the chart below.
- Ask yourself questions to think about what elements are in the nonfiction texts you read.

Text Element	What Is This Element?	Guiding Questions
Purpose for Reading	This is your reason for reading the text. Sometimes you read: • to learn about a topic • for entertainment • to find specific facts about a topic	• Why am I reading this text? • What do I want to learn from the text? • Does the text match my reason for reading? • Is the author's purpose to entertain, inform, argue, or teach?
Major Ideas	These are the most important messages in the text. They are the things that the author wants you to understand.	• What main ideas is the author sharing? • How are these ideas being shared?
Supporting Details	These are the details that help you understand the main idea(s) in the text.	• What are the supporting details for each major idea? • How are the supporting details shared?
Visuals and Graphics	These are pictures or graphics that help you understand what the text means. They include: • illustrations and photos • graphs, diagrams, and tables • charts and timelines	• What pictures or graphics does the author use to give me information? • Do the pictures or graphics tell about major ideas or supporting details? • Do the pictures or graphics help me understand information from the text?
Vocabulary	These are words that you must understand in order to know what the text is about.	• What key words are used to tell about major ideas or supporting details? • Does the text have any signal words? • What words in the text are bold or italicized?

Name: _____

Five Structures of Nonfiction Text

A **structure** is how a text is organized and how the main ideas are shared.

- Thinking about the text structure helps you to understand what the major idea of the text is.
- Signal words help you identify what kind of structure a text has. They also help you find details that support the major ideas.
- Nonfiction texts follow one of the structures listed in the chart below.

Text Structures	What Is This Element?	Signal Words
Main Idea and Details	A major idea is supported by details and examples. Signal words are in sentences that have supporting details.	• for instance, for example, such as, another, also, in addition
Time Order	A major idea is supported by details. The major idea and details are in a certain order so the text makes sense.	• at, first, during, next, last, before, after, then, while, finally, following, when
Compare and Contrast	The major idea is that two or more things are alike in some ways and different in others. The major idea is supported by details and examples.	• but, different, same, however, as well as, both, while, instead of
Cause and Effect	A major idea offers a cause, or the reason something happened, and an effect, or what happens as a result. The cause-and-effect structure also has details and examples.	• because, in order to, effects of, for this reason, if...then, causes, allow
Question and Answer	The major idea is written as a question. Supporting details answer the question.	• who? what? where? when? why? how?

Science Article
Text Structure: Compare and Contrast

Big, Wild Cats!

Lesson Objective   Students will explain how a tiger moves, eats, and lives in the forests and jungles of Asia.

Content Knowledge   Animals depend on the land, water, and air to live and grow.

Lesson Preparation

Reproduce and distribute one copy of the article, dictionary page, and activity pages to each student.

SCIENCE
Big, Wild Cats!

Name: _____

Big, Wild Cats!

The roar of a lion or a tiger can make a person shake with fear. Lions and tigers are close relatives, but they have differences, too.

Where Lions and Tigers Live

These big cats both live in the wild. However, they live in different parts of the world. Lions live in the grasslands of Africa. Their sandy-colored fur blends in with the tall yellow grasses. Tigers live in forests and jungles in Asia. Their orange fur has dark stripes that help them hide among trees. No two tigers have the same pattern of stripes.

The weather is hot where lions and tigers live. Lions like to stay dry. They go into water only if they have to. However, tigers are good swimmers. They may swim across rivers to hunt. They also go into water to cool off.

How Big Cats Live

Both kinds of big cats live and hunt in an area that covers many miles. This area is their *territory*. Lions live in family groups called *prides*. A pride has males, females, and their cubs. Each pride has its own territory. Lions roar to guard their territory. An adult lion's roar can be heard up to five miles away.

Lions live in family groups called prides.

Unlike lions, tigers do not live in groups. A mother tiger raises her cubs without their father. The cubs stay with their mother for only two years. Then they live alone in their own territory.

Reading Comprehension: Nonfiction • EMC 3263 • © Evan-Moor Corporation

14

...are in danger. Many lions die from sicknesses caused by hot weather and not enough water. Also, lions are losing their territories because people are using the land to grow food. Long ago, lions were found in Africa, Asia, and Europe. Today, they live only in Africa and in one forest in India.

Some people hunt tigers for their skin and other parts. Tigers are losing their territories as forests are cut down. Tigers used to live in many parts of Asia. Today, they live only in small areas. Many people are working to save lions and tigers.

Unlike lions, tigers hunt alone. This tiger is creeping toward its prey.

© Evan-Moor Corporation • EMC 3263 • Reading Comprehension: Nonfiction

15

1 Read Aloud the Article

Read aloud *Big, Wild Cats!* Have students follow along silently as you read.

2 Introduce the Vocabulary

Content Vocabulary
Read aloud the Content Vocabulary words and definitions. Point out that *grasslands* is a compound word that contains the words *grass* and *lands.* The two words give clues about the meaning of the word. Explain that *sandy-colored* is another compound word used in the article. It is a describing word that has a hyphen connecting its two word parts. Discuss definitions and usage as needed.

Academic Vocabulary
Next, read aloud the Academic Vocabulary words and definitions. Discuss definitions and usage as needed. Then read these context sentences from the article, emphasizing the Academic Vocabulary words:

*Lions and tigers are close **relatives**, but they have differences, too.*

*A pride has **males**, **females**, and their cubs.*

*An **adult** lion's roar can be heard up to five miles away.*

3 Students Read the Article

Have students read the article independently, with a partner, or in small groups. After students read, guide a discussion about the article. Direct students' attention to graphic elements or visual aids.

4 Identify Information

Explain that students will locate important information in the article. After students complete the activity, allow time for a question-and-answer session.

5 Answer Questions

Encourage students to use the article to answer the questions and/or check their answers.

6 Apply Vocabulary

Have students reread the article before they complete the vocabulary activity. Optional: Have students mark each vocabulary word as they read.

7 Examine Text Structure

Read aloud the Compare and Contrast description and Signal Words. Then have students read the article again, underlining signal words in red. Then guide students in completing the activity.

8 Write About It:
A Tiger's Life

Have students complete the writing activity independently or in small groups.

Name: _____

Big, Wild Cats!

The roar of a lion or a tiger can make a person shake with fear. Lions and tigers are close relatives, but they have differences, too.

Where Lions and Tigers Live

These big cats both live in the wild. However, they live in different parts of the world. Lions live in the grasslands of Africa. Their sandy-colored fur blends in with the tall yellow grasses. Tigers live in forests and jungles in Asia. Their orange fur has dark stripes that help them hide among trees. No two tigers have the same pattern of stripes.

The weather is hot where lions and tigers live. Lions like to stay dry. They go into water only if they have to. However, tigers are good swimmers. They may swim across rivers to hunt. They also go into water to cool off.

How Big Cats Live

Both kinds of big cats live and hunt in an area that covers many miles. This area is their *territory*. Lions live in family groups called *prides.* A pride has males, females, and their cubs. Each pride has its own territory. Lions roar to guard their territory. An adult lion's roar can be heard up to five miles away.

Lions live in family groups called prides.

Unlike lions, tigers do not live in groups. A mother tiger raises her cubs without their father. The cubs stay with their mother for only two years. Then they live alone in their own territory.

How Lions and Tigers Catch Their Food

Lions and tigers are meat eaters. Both kinds of cats are strong hunters that have sharp teeth and claws. Lions and tigers both creep up on their prey and attack by surprise. Female lions do most of the hunting. They may work as a team to hunt animals that are faster than they are. Unlike lions, tigers hunt alone.

Dangers to Big Cats

Both lions and tigers are in danger. Many lions die from sicknesses caused by hot weather and not enough water. Also, lions are losing their territories because people are using the land to grow food. Long ago, lions were found in Africa, Asia, and Europe. Today, they live only in Africa and in one forest in India.

Unlike lions, tigers hunt alone. This tiger is creeping toward its prey.

Some people hunt tigers for their skin and other parts. Tigers are losing their territories as forests are cut down. Tigers used to live in many parts of Asia. Today, they live only in small areas. Many people are working to save lions and tigers.

Dictionary

Content Vocabulary

attack
to try to hurt or kill

forests
areas of land where many trees grow

grasslands
areas of land that are covered with grasses but not trees or bushes

jungles
areas of land that are thickly covered with bushes, trees, and vines

prey
animals that are hunted and eaten by other animals

Academic Vocabulary

relatives
members of the same family or animal group

males
animals that can be the father of young

females
animals that can be the mother of young

adult
a full-grown animal

Write a sentence that includes a vocabulary word.

_____

_____

Name: _____

Identify Information

You can understand a text better if you read it more than once. Look for the following information as you read the article again. Put a check mark in the box after you complete each task.

		I did it!
✏	Highlight any words that describe where lions live.	☐
☐	Draw a box around any words that describe where tigers live.	☐
○	Circle four words that describe the fur of lions and tigers.	☐
—	Draw a line under the sentence that explains how tigers cool off.	☐
[ ]	Put brackets around the sentences that explain what a territory is.	☐
★	Draw a star next to the paragraph about how lions and tigers hunt.	☐
✖	Put an X next to each paragraph that explains why people are working to save lions and tigers.	☐
▲	Draw a triangle next to any information that surprised or interested you.	☐
?	Put a question mark beside any words or sentences you don't understand.	☐

Name: _____

Answer Questions

Use information from the article to answer each question.

1. Lions live in Africa's grasslands, but tigers live in _____.
   - Ⓐ Africa's forests
   - Ⓑ Asia's grasslands
   - Ⓒ Asia's jungles
   - Ⓓ Africa and Asia

2. Both lions and tigers have _____.
   - Ⓐ prides
   - Ⓑ their own territories
   - Ⓒ dark stripes
   - Ⓓ sandy-colored fur

3. When they hunt, both kinds of big cats _____.
   - Ⓐ attack by surprise
   - Ⓑ roar loudly
   - Ⓒ work as a team
   - Ⓓ work alone

4. How does a lion's fur help it live in the wild?

   _____

   _____

5. How does a tiger's fur help it live in the wild?

   _____

   _____

Name: _____

Apply Vocabulary

Use a word from the word box to complete each sentence.

Word Box

females	grasslands	prey
jungles	relatives	males
attack	forests	adult

1. Lions blend in with Africa's _____ because of the color of their fur.

2. Among lions, _____ do most of the hunting.

3. Tigers and lions are both cats, which makes them _____.

4. Animals that live in forests and _____ are food for tigers.

5. A team of female lions may work together to hunt _____.

6. Among tigers, the _____ do not help raise their own cubs.

7. An _____ lion's roar can be heard miles away.

8. Tigers can be found in _____ and jungles throughout Asia.

9. Lions and tigers use sharp teeth and claws to _____ their prey.

Compare and Contrast

....

A text that has a **compare-and-contrast** structure is about two main ideas. It tells how the two ideas are alike (compares). It also tells how the two ideas are different (contrasts).

Authors use these signal words to create a **compare-and-contrast** structure:

Signal Words

both	today	but
long ago	however	unlike

1. The first paragraph tells us that the article will compare and contrast what two things?

   _____

2. Write the sentence that tells how tigers are different from lions in the way they live.

   _____

   _____

3. Are lions and tigers alike or different in what they eat? Write the sentence from the article that tells you how they are similar or different.

   _____

   _____

Name: _____

Write About It

Explain how a tiger moves, eats, and lives in the forests and jungles of Asia. Include facts and details from the article.

A Tiger's Life

_____

_____

_____

_____

_____

_____

_____

_____

_____

_____

_____

_____

_____

_____

Plants of the Rainforest

Lesson Objective
Students will write an argument for whether or not it is important for people to protect the rainforests.

Content Knowledge
Rainfall affects the types of plants found in a region. Plants in turn affect the air and weather. They provide products useful to people.

Lesson Preparation

Reproduce and distribute one copy of the article, dictionary page, and activity pages to each student.

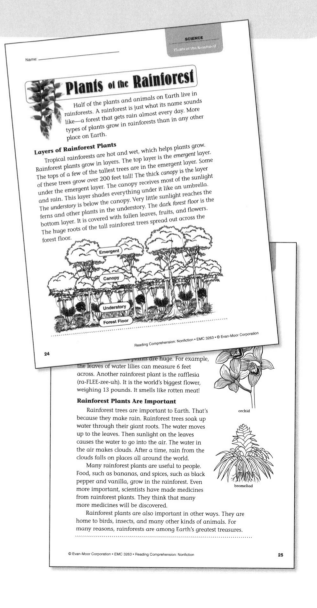

1 Read Aloud the Article

Read aloud *Plants of the Rainforest*. Have students follow along silently as you read.

2 Introduce the Vocabulary

Content Vocabulary

Read aloud the Content Vocabulary words and definitions. Point out that *scientists* has the suffix *-ist,* which means "a person who studies a certain subject" (in this case, science). Explain that the words for many types of scientists also include this suffix. For example, a *zoologist* studies animals, a *chemist* studies chemicals, and a *geologist* studies rocks. Discuss definitions and usage as needed.

Academic Vocabulary

Next, read aloud the Academic Vocabulary words and definitions. Discuss definitions and usage as needed. Then read these context sentences from the article, emphasizing the Academic Vocabulary words:

*Rainforest trees **soak** up water through their giant roots.*

*Food, such as bananas, and **spices,** such as black pepper and vanilla, grow in the rainforest.*

*Even more important, scientists have made **medicines** from rainforest plants.*

*For many reasons, rainforests are among Earth's greatest **treasures**.*

3 Students Read the Article

Have students read the article independently, with a partner, or in small groups. After students read, guide a discussion about the article. Direct students' attention to graphic elements or visual aids.

4 Identify Information

Explain that students will locate important information in the article. After students complete the activity, allow time for a question-and-answer session.

5 Answer Questions

Encourage students to use the article to answer the questions and/or check their answers.

6 Apply Vocabulary

Have students reread the article before they complete the vocabulary activity. Optional: Have students mark each vocabulary word as they read.

7 Examine Text Structure

Read aloud the Main Idea and Details description and Signal Words. Then have students read the article again, underlining signal words in red. Then guide students in completing the activity.

8 Write About It:
Protecting Rainforests

Have students complete the writing activity independently or in small groups.

Name: _____

Plants of the Rainforest

Half of the plants and animals on Earth live in rainforests. A rainforest is just what its name sounds like—a forest that gets rain almost every day. More types of plants grow in rainforests than in any other place on Earth.

Layers of Rainforest Plants

Tropical rainforests are hot and wet, which helps plants grow. Rainforest plants grow in layers. The top layer is the *emergent* layer. The tops of a few of the tallest trees are in the emergent layer. Some of these trees grow over 200 feet tall! The thick *canopy* is the layer under the emergent layer. The canopy receives most of the sunlight and rain. This layer shades everything under it like an umbrella. The *understory* is below the canopy. Very little sunlight reaches the ferns and other plants in the understory. The dark *forest floor* is the bottom layer. It is covered with fallen leaves, fruits, and flowers. The huge roots of the tall rainforest trees spread out across the forest floor.

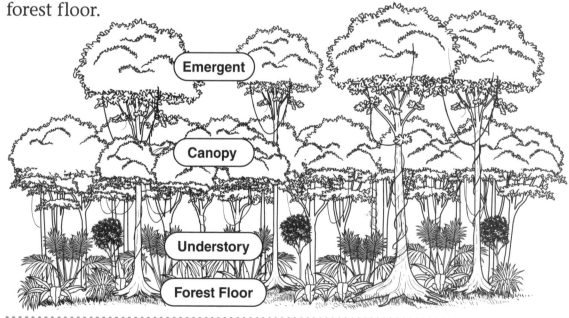

Emergent

Canopy

Understory

Forest Floor

Types of Rainforest Plants

Plants of many sizes, shapes, and colors grow in rainforests. Thousands of different kinds of orchids (OR-kidz) grow on tree trunks high up in the rainforest canopy. Their roots take water from the air instead of the soil. Bromeliads (bro-MEE-lee-adz) grow on trees in the canopy as well. They need lots of light. Their long, narrow leaves form pockets to catch rainwater.

Many rainforest plants are huge. For example, the leaves of water lilies can measure 6 feet across. Another rainforest plant is the rafflesia (ra-FLEE-zee-uh). It is the world's biggest flower, weighing 13 pounds. It smells like rotten meat!

Rainforest Plants Are Important

Rainforest trees are important to Earth. That's because they make rain. Rainforest trees soak up water through their giant roots. The water moves up to the leaves. Then sunlight on the leaves causes the water to go into the air. The water in the air makes clouds. After a time, rain from the clouds falls on places all around the world.

Many rainforest plants are useful to people. Food, such as bananas, and spices, such as black pepper and vanilla, grow in the rainforest. Even more important, scientists have made medicines from rainforest plants. They think that many more medicines will be discovered.

Rainforest plants are also important in other ways. They are home to birds, insects, and many other kinds of animals. For many reasons, rainforests are among Earth's greatest treasures.

orchid

bromeliad

Name: _____

Dictionary

Content Vocabulary

bromeliad (bro-MEE-lee-ad)
a rainforest plant that can live off water in the air instead of water in the soil

layers
something on or between other things

orchids (OR-kidz)
plants with bright flowers that have odd shapes

rainforest
a thick forest in an area that is often hot and rainy

scientists
people who study science

tropical
having to do with a hot, wet part of Earth

Academic Vocabulary

soak
to take in a liquid, such as through roots

spices
flavorings for food that are made from plant parts

medicines
things that are used to treat or cure sickness

treasures
things that are special or that have value

Write a sentence that includes a vocabulary word.

_____

_____

Identify Information

You can understand a text better if you read it more than once. Look for the following information as you read the article again. Put a check mark in the box after you complete each task.

		I did it!
🖍️	Highlight one sentence in the first paragraph that tells what a rainforest is like.	☐
—	Draw a line under two sentences that give details about the forest floor.	☐
○	Circle a detail about the rainforest water lily.	☐
★	Draw a star beside the paragraph that explains how the rainforest makes rain.	☐
✖	Put an X next to the paragraph that explains why rainforest plants are useful to people.	☐
[ ]	Put brackets around the sentence that tells how scientists have used rainforest plants.	☐
!	Put an exclamation point beside any information that surprised or interested you.	☐
?	Put a question mark beside any words or sentences you don't understand.	☐

Answer Questions

Use information from the article to answer each question.

1. The rainforest layer that shades things like an umbrella is the _____.
   - Ⓐ forest floor
   - Ⓑ canopy
   - Ⓒ understory
   - Ⓓ emergent

2. The _____ plant has the world's largest flower.
   - Ⓐ orchid
   - Ⓑ water lily
   - Ⓒ bromeliad
   - Ⓓ rafflesia

3. Plants in the understory _____.
   - Ⓐ receive little sunlight
   - Ⓑ are taller than the canopy
   - Ⓒ grow over 200 feet tall
   - Ⓓ are covered with fallen leaves

4. Explain why rainforest trees are important to the weather on Earth.

   _____

   _____

5. Would a rafflesia make a good gift for most people? Why or why not?

   _____

   _____

Name: _____

Apply Vocabulary

Use a word from the word box to complete each sentence.

Word Box				
medicines	spices	layers	rainforest	bromeliad
treasures	scientists	tropical	soak	orchids

1. The bottom two _____ of the rainforest are the understory and the forest floor.

2. The roots of rainforest plants _____ up water.

3. Black pepper and vanilla are two kinds of _____.

4. _____ have discovered many important ways to use rainforest plants.

5. A _____ place has hot, wet weather.

6. New kinds of _____ may be made from rainforest plants.

7. Rainforests are one of the world's _____ because they help people and animals.

8. There are thousands of different kinds of _____.

9. Like the orchid, the _____ is a plant that grows in the canopy of the rainforest.

10. A _____ is home to birds, insects, plants, and animals.

Main Idea and Details

A text that has a **main idea and details** structure mentions a main idea and gives several details about it. The details can be given in any order.

Authors use these signal words to create a **main idea and details** structure:

Signal Words

another	also	such as
for example	even more important	as well

1. The title and the first paragraph tell us that the main idea of the article is

   _____

2. What are the names of the layers of the rainforest? In what order did the author write about the layers?

   _____

   _____

3. Besides rain, what other kinds of things from the rainforest help us?

   _____

4. What do the headings in the article tell us?

   _____

   _____

Write About It

Is it really important for people to protect the rainforests? Write an argument for why or why not. Include facts and details from the article.

Protecting Rainforests

_____

_____

_____

_____

_____

_____

_____

_____

_____

_____

_____

_____

_____

_____

Two Climates

Lesson Objective	Students will write and support an opinion about which climate they would prefer to live in: Seattle's climate or San Diego's climate.
Content Knowledge	"Climate" describes a range of an area's typical weather conditions.

Lesson Preparation

Reproduce and distribute one copy of the article, dictionary page, and activity pages to each student.

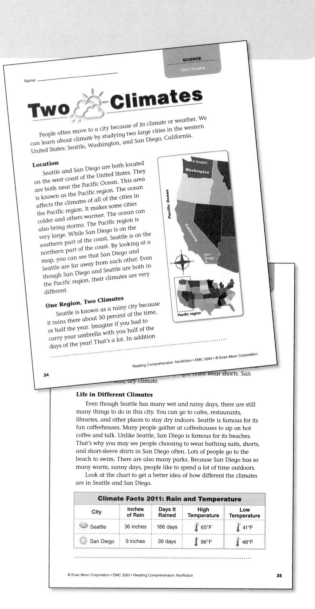

1 Read Aloud the Article

Read aloud *Two Climates.* Have students follow along silently as you read.

2 Introduce the Vocabulary

Content Vocabulary
Read aloud the Content Vocabulary words and definitions. Explain that *degrees* and *Fahrenheit* are words we use to show how we measure temperature in the United States. Discuss definitions and usage as needed.

Academic Vocabulary
Next, read aloud the Academic Vocabulary words and definitions. Discuss definitions and usage as needed. Then read these context sentences from the article, emphasizing the Academic Vocabulary words:

*This area is known as the Pacific **region**.*

*This is because Seattle's **average** temperature is 52 degrees Fahrenheit, which is quite chilly.*

*You can go to **cafes**, restaurants, libraries, and other places to stay dry indoors.*

3 Students Read the Article

Have students read the article independently, with a partner, or in small groups. After students read, guide a discussion about the article. Direct students' attention to graphic elements or visual aids.

4 Identify Information

Explain that students will locate important information in the article. After students complete the activity, allow time for a question-and-answer session.

5 Answer Questions

Encourage students to use the article to answer the questions and/or check their answers.

6 Apply Vocabulary

Have students reread the article before they complete the vocabulary activity. Optional: Have students mark each vocabulary word as they read.

7 Examine Text Structure

Read aloud the Compare and Contrast description and Signal Words. Then have students read the article again, underlining signal words in red. Then guide students in completing the activity.

8 Write About It: *Where I Would Live*

Have students complete the writing activity independently or in small groups.

Name: _____

Two  Climates

People often move to a city because of its climate or weather. We can learn about climate by studying two large cities in the western United States: Seattle, Washington, and San Diego, California.

Location

Seattle and San Diego are both located on the west coast of the United States. They are both near the Pacific Ocean. This area is known as the Pacific region. The ocean affects the climates of all of the cities in the Pacific region. It makes some cities colder and others warmer. The ocean can also bring storms. The Pacific region is very large. While San Diego is on the southern part of the coast, Seattle is on the northern part of the coast. By looking at a map, you can see that San Diego and Seattle are far away from each other. Even though San Diego and Seattle are both in the Pacific region, their climates are very different.

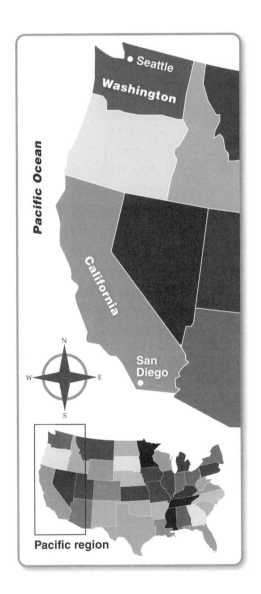

Pacific region

One Region, Two Climates

Seattle is known as a rainy city because it rains there about 50 percent of the time, or half the year. Imagine if you had to carry your umbrella with you half of the days of the year! That's a lot. In addition to carrying an umbrella, you'd want to wear a sweater or a light jacket most days of the year. This is because Seattle's average temperature is 52 degrees Fahrenheit, which is quite chilly. Seattle's summers are warm enough to wear shorts, but they are not very hot. So Seattle has a wet climate that's not too hot or too cold. Unlike Seattle, San Diego has many warm days during the year. San Diego is known as a sunny city. It has dry air and less rain than Seattle. San Diego's average temperature is 63 degrees Fahrenheit, which is warmer than Seattle's. San Diego's summers are so hot that people often wear shorts. San Diego has a warm, dry climate.

Life in Different Climates

Even though Seattle has many wet and rainy days, there are still many things to do in this city. You can go to cafes, restaurants, libraries, and other places to stay dry indoors. Seattle is famous for its fun coffeehouses. Many people gather at coffeehouses to sip on hot coffee and talk. Unlike Seattle, San Diego is famous for its beaches. That's why you may see people choosing to wear bathing suits, shorts, and short-sleeve shirts in San Diego often. Lots of people go to the beach to swim. There are also many parks. Because San Diego has so many warm, sunny days, people like to spend a lot of time outdoors.

Look at the chart to get a better idea of how different the climates are in Seattle and San Diego.

Climate Facts 2011: Rain and Temperature				
City	Inches of Rain	Days It Rained	High Temperature	Low Temperature
Seattle	36 inches	166 days	65°F	41°F
San Diego	9 inches	39 days	96°F	48°F

Name: _____

Dictionary

Content Vocabulary

climate
the weather patterns in an area

coast
seashore; land next to the sea

degrees (°)
units of measure for
temperature

Fahrenheit
a system for measuring
temperature in which water
freezes at 32° and boils at 212°

temperature
a measure of the amount
of heat in something

Academic Vocabulary

region
a certain place, space, or area

average
usual; most common

cafes
coffeehouses; restaurants that
serve coffee

Write a sentence that includes a vocabulary word.

_____

_____

Name: _____

Identify Information

You can understand a text better if you read it more than once. Look for the following information as you read the article again. Put a check mark in the box after you complete each task.

		I did it!
—	Draw a line under the sentence that tells which coast Seattle and San Diego are located on.	☐
	Highlight any sentences that mention the Pacific region.	☐
[ ]	Put brackets around the sentence that explains why Seattle is known as a rainy city.	☐
✖	Put an X next to the sentence that tells about Seattle's summer climate.	☐
◯	Circle the average temperatures of Seattle and San Diego.	☐
★	In the chart, draw a star beside the number of rainy days San Diego had in 2011.	☐
!	Put an exclamation point beside any information that surprised or interested you.	☐
?	Put a question mark beside any words or sentences you don't understand.	☐

Name: _____

Answer Questions

Use information from the article to answer each question.

1. Both San Diego and Seattle are _____.

   Ⓐ popular for cafes

   Ⓑ on the northern part of the coast

   Ⓒ on the southern part of the coast

   Ⓓ in the Pacific region

2. In 2011, San Diego received _____ of rain.

   Ⓐ 9 inches

   Ⓑ 36 inches

   Ⓒ 48 inches

   Ⓓ 166 days

3. The Pacific region got its name from being near _____.

   Ⓐ the United States of America

   Ⓑ the Pacific Ocean

   Ⓒ Washington

   Ⓓ California

4. List San Diego's average temperature and Seattle's average temperature.

   _____

   _____

5. Study the chart. Then explain how Seattle's climate was different from San Diego's climate in 2011.

   _____

   _____

Reading Comprehension: Nonfiction • EMC 3263 • © Evan-Moor Corporation

Name: _____

Apply Vocabulary

Use a word from the word box to complete each sentence.

Word Box

coast	average	degrees	Fahrenheit
cafes	temperature	climate	region

1. You can get different flavors of coffee at most _____ in Seattle.

2. Both California and Washington are in the Pacific _____.

3. San Diego's _____ is warm and dry.

4. In the United States, _____ is measured in degrees Fahrenheit.

5. Beaches are often found on a country's _____.

6. San Diego has a higher _____ temperature in the summer than Seattle.

7. The temperature 17°C is equal to 63 degrees _____.

8. We measure temperature using _____.

Name: _____

Compare and Contrast

A text that has a **compare-and-contrast** structure is about two main ideas. It tells how the two ideas are alike (compares). It also tells how the two ideas are different (contrasts).

Authors use these signal words to create a **compare-and-contrast** structure:

Signal Words

both	but	unlike
same	while	different

1. Which city is famous for its beaches?

   _____

2. Write two ways that Seattle and San Diego are the same.

   a. _____

   b. _____

3. Write two ways that Seattle and San Diego are different.

   a. _____

   _____

   b. _____

   _____

Write About It

Would you rather live in San Diego's climate or Seattle's climate? Write your opinion, and explain why you feel that way. Include facts and details from the article.

Where I Would Live

_____

_____

_____

_____

_____

_____

_____

_____

_____

_____

_____

_____

_____

_____

_____

Social Studies Article
Text Structure: Main Idea and Details

It's a Grand Old Flag

Lesson Objective   Students will explain how the U.S. got its flag and how and why people show respect to the flag.

Content Knowledge   The United States Flag Code sets standards for showing respect for the flag.

Lesson Preparation

Reproduce and distribute one copy of the article, dictionary page, and activity pages to each student.

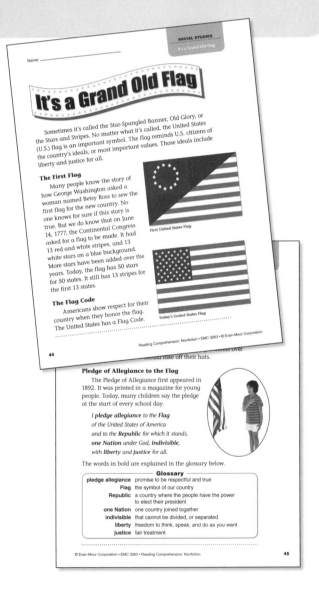

1 Read Aloud the Article

Read aloud *It's a Grand Old Flag*. Have students follow along silently as you read.

2 Introduce the Vocabulary

Content Vocabulary
Read aloud the Content Vocabulary words and definitions. Explain that the *Continental Congress* was a group of people from the thirteen colonies who helped make rules and laws. Discuss definitions and usage as needed.

Academic Vocabulary
Next, read aloud the Academic Vocabulary words and definitions. Discuss definitions and usage as needed. Then read these context sentences from the article, emphasizing the Academic Vocabulary words:

The flag reminds U.S. citizens of the country's **ideals**, *or most important values.*

The United States has a Flag **Code**.

It is **proper** *to* **display** *a flag in a place of honor.*

3 Students Read the Article

Have students read the article independently, with a partner, or in small groups. After students read, guide a discussion about the article. Direct students' attention to graphic elements or visual aids.

4 Identify Information

Explain that students will locate important information in the article. After students complete the activity, allow time for a question-and-answer session.

5 Answer Questions

Encourage students to use the article to answer the questions and/or check their answers.

6 Apply Vocabulary

Have students reread the article before they complete the vocabulary activity. Optional: Have students mark each vocabulary word as they read.

7 Examine Text Structure

Read aloud the Main Idea and Details description and Signal Words. Then have students read the article again, underlining signal words in red. Then guide students in completing the activity.

8 Write About It:
Honoring American Ideals

Have students complete the writing activity independently or in small groups.

It's a Grand Old Flag

Sometimes it's called the Star-Spangled Banner, Old Glory, or the Stars and Stripes. No matter what it's called, the United States (U.S.) flag is an important symbol. The flag reminds U.S. citizens of the country's ideals, or most important values. Those ideals include liberty and justice for all.

The First Flag

Many people know the story of how George Washington asked a woman named Betsy Ross to sew the first flag for the new country. No one knows for sure if this story is true. But we do know that on June 14, 1777, the Continental Congress asked for a flag to be made. It had 13 red and white stripes, and 13 white stars on a blue background. More stars have been added over the years. Today, the flag has 50 stars for 50 states. It still has 13 stripes for the first 13 states.

First United States Flag

The Flag Code

Americans show respect for their country when they honor the flag. The United States has a Flag Code.

Today's United States Flag

The Flag Code is a guide for treating the flag with respect. There are many rules the Flag Code says people should follow. For example, the flag's stars should always be in the top left corner. It is proper to display a flag in a place of honor. Indoors, it should be placed to the right of a person giving a speech. Outdoors at night, the flag should have a light shining on it. The Flag Code also says everyone should face the flag when a flag passes by in a parade. In addition, people in military uniforms should salute the flag, and other people should place their right hands over their hearts. Also, men should take off their hats.

Pledge of Allegiance to the Flag

The Pledge of Allegiance first appeared in 1892. It was printed in a magazine for young people. Today, many children say the pledge at the start of every school day.

I **pledge allegiance** to the **Flag**

of the United States of America

and to the **Republic** for which it stands,

one Nation under God, **indivisible**,

with **liberty** and **justice** for all.

The words in bold are explained in the glossary below.

Glossary	
pledge allegiance	promise to be respectful and true
Flag	the symbol of our country
Republic	a country where the people have the power to elect their president
one Nation	one country joined together
indivisible	that cannot be divided, or separated
liberty	freedom to think, speak, and do as you want
justice	fair treatment

Dictionary

Content Vocabulary

allegiance
respect for someone or
something

citizens
people who, by law, belong
to a country

Continental Congress
the main government of the
United States when it was
becoming a country

pledge
to promise; a promise

salute
to show a sign of respect with
a special hand motion

symbol
a thing that stands for
something else

united
joined together

Academic Vocabulary

ideals
ideas about what would
be perfect or best

code
a set of rules to be followed

proper
correct

display
to put something in a place
where people can see it

Write a sentence that includes a vocabulary word.

_____

_____

Identify Information

You can understand a text better if you read it more than once. Look for the following information as you read the article again. Put a check mark in the box after you complete each task.

		I did it!
◯	Circle three names for the flag of the United States.	☐
✏	Highlight the sentence that tells what ideals the flag stands for.	☐
[ ]	Put brackets around the sentence that describes what the first flag looked like.	☐
✖	Put an X next to the heading of the paragraph that explains how to treat the flag with respect.	☐
—	Draw a line under the sentence that explains how to display the flag at night.	☐
★	Draw a star beside the paragraph about the Pledge of Allegiance.	☐
!	Put an exclamation point beside any information that surprised or interested you.	☐
?	Put a question mark beside any words or sentences you don't understand.	☐

Answer Questions

Use information from the article to answer each question.

1. Old Glory _____.
   - Ⓐ is another name for George Washington
   - Ⓑ is another name for the United States flag
   - Ⓒ was made in 1892
   - Ⓓ sewed the first flag

2. The Flag Code _____.
   - Ⓐ stands for liberty and justice
   - Ⓑ has 13 red and white stripes
   - Ⓒ is another name for the pledge
   - Ⓓ tells how to honor the flag

3. The word *justice* means _____.
   - Ⓐ a promise
   - Ⓑ a set of rules
   - Ⓒ fair treatment
   - Ⓓ a sign of respect

4. Describe the first flag of the United States.

   _____

   _____

5. Describe the flag of the United States as it is today.

   _____

   _____

Reading Comprehension: Nonfiction • EMC 3263 • © Evan-Moor Corporation

Name: _____

Apply Vocabulary

Use a word from the word box to complete each sentence.

Word Box

display	proper	ideals	citizens
pledge	united	symbol	salute
code	allegiance	Continental Congress	

1. The _____ States of America has ideals.

2. People _____ the flag with a hand motion.

3. The flag of the United States is an important _____.

4. The flag stands for the _____ of liberty and justice.

5. You pledge _____ to the United States flag.

6. It is _____ to respect the United States flag.

7. It is important to follow the _____ to show the flag respect.

8. People can _____ the U.S. flag indoors or outdoors.

9. Students in the U.S. _____ allegiance to the flag daily.

10. The _____ asked for a flag to be made in 1777.

11. The United States flag reminds _____ of the country's ideals.

Main Idea and Details

A text that has a **main idea and details** structure mentions a main idea and gives several details about it. The details can be given in any order.

Authors use these signal words to create a **main idea and details** structure:

> **Signal Words**
>
> | for example | also | for instance |
> |---|---|---|
> | include | other | in addition |

1. The first paragraph tells us that the main idea of the article is

   _____

2. Each paragraph gives details about the flag. List the paragraph headings.

   _____

   _____

   _____

3. Write two sentences from the article that use **main idea and details** signal words.

   a. _____

   _____

   b. _____

   _____

Write About It

···

Explain how the United States got its flag. Also explain how and why people show respect to the flag. Include facts and details from the article.

Honoring American Ideals

_____

_____

_____

_____

_____

_____

_____

_____

_____

_____

_____

_____

_____

Social Studies Article
Text Structure: Time Order

The Mystery of Mesa Verde

Lesson Objective   Students will explain what archaeologists know about how the Ancestral Pueblo people lived and how archaeologists gained the information that they have.

Content Knowledge   Archaeologists uncover ancient cities to discover how people once lived.

Lesson Preparation

Reproduce and distribute one copy of the article, dictionary page, and activity pages to each student.

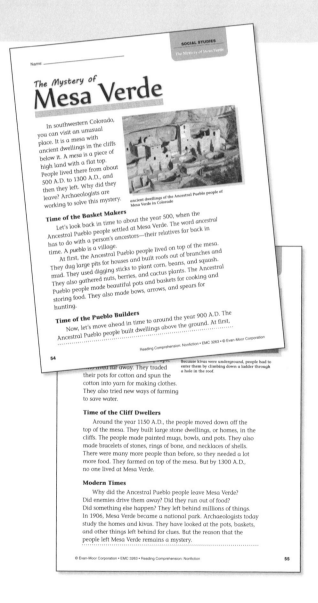

SOCIAL STUDIES
The Mystery of Mesa Verde

Name: _____

The Mystery of Mesa Verde

In southwestern Colorado, you can visit an unusual place. It is a mesa with ancient dwellings in the cliffs below it. A *mesa* is a piece of high land with a flat top. People lived there from about 500 A.D. to 1300 A.D., and then they left. Why did they leave? Archaeologists are working to solve this mystery.

ancient dwellings of the Ancestral Pueblo people of Mesa Verde in Colorado

Time of the Basket Makers

Let's look back in time to about the year 500, when the Ancestral Pueblo people settled at Mesa Verde. The word *ancestral* has to do with a person's ancestors—their relatives far back in time. A *pueblo* is a village.

At first, the Ancestral Pueblo people lived on top of the mesa. They dug large pits for houses and built roofs out of branches and mud. They used digging sticks to plant corn, beans, and squash. They also gathered nuts, berries, and cactus plants. The Ancestral Pueblo people made beautiful pots and baskets for cooking and storing food. They also made bows, arrows, and spears for hunting.

Time of the Pueblo Builders

Now, let's move ahead in time to around the year 900 A.D. The Ancestral Pueblo people built dwellings above the ground. At first,

Reading Comprehension: Nonfiction • EMC 3263 • © Evan-Moor Corporation

54

...lived far away. They traded their pots for cotton and spun the cotton into yarn for making clothes. They also tried new ways of farming to save water.

Because kivas were underground, people had to enter them by climbing down a ladder through a hole in the roof.

Time of the Cliff Dwellers

Around the year 1150 A.D., the people moved down off the top of the mesa. They built large stone dwellings, or homes, in the cliffs. The people made painted mugs, bowls, and pots. They also made bracelets of stones, rings of bone, and necklaces of shells. There were many more people than before, so they needed a lot more food. They farmed on top of the mesa. But by 1300 A.D., no one lived at Mesa Verde.

Modern Times

Why did the Ancestral Pueblo people leave Mesa Verde? Did enemies drive them away? Did they run out of food? Did something else happen? They left behind millions of things. In 1906, Mesa Verde became a national park. Archaeologists today study the homes and kivas. They have looked at the pots, baskets, and other things left behind for clues. But the reason that the people left Mesa Verde remains a mystery.

© Evan-Moor Corporation • EMC 3263 • Reading Comprehension: Nonfiction   55

1 Read Aloud the Article

Read aloud *The Mystery of Mesa Verde.* Have students follow along silently as you read.

2 Introduce the Vocabulary

Content Vocabulary
Read aloud the Content Vocabulary words and definitions. Point out that many words in the article are borrowed from Spanish, including *adobe* (to plaster), *pueblo* (village), *mesa* (table), and *verde* (green). Tell students that *Mesa Verde* is pronounced MAY-suh VAIR-day. Also point out that *kiva* (KEE-vuh) comes from the language of the Hopi people, who live in northeastern Arizona today. Discuss definitions and usage as needed.

Academic Vocabulary
Next, read aloud the Academic Vocabulary words and definitions. Discuss definitions and usage as needed. Then read these context sentences from the article, emphasizing the Academic Vocabulary words:

*In southwestern Colorado, you can visit an **unusual** place.*

*Their homes had kivas—round underground rooms used for **gatherings**.*

*But the reason that the people left Mesa Verde remains a **mystery**.*

3 Students Read the Article

Have students read the article independently, with a partner, or in small groups. After students read, guide a discussion about the article. Direct students' attention to graphic elements or visual aids.

4 Identify Information

Explain that students will locate important information in the article. After students complete the activity, allow time for a question-and-answer session.

5 Answer Questions

Encourage students to use the article to answer the questions and/or check their answers.

6 Apply Vocabulary

Have students reread the article before they complete the vocabulary activity. Optional: Have students mark each vocabulary word as they read.

7 Examine Text Structure

Read aloud the Time Order description and Signal Words. Then have students read the article again, underlining signal words in red. Then guide students in completing the activity.

8 Write About It:
Leaving Home

Have students complete the writing activity independently or in small groups.

Name: _____

The Mystery of Mesa Verde

In southwestern Colorado, you can visit an unusual place. It is a mesa with ancient dwellings in the cliffs below it. A *mesa* is a piece of high land with a flat top. People lived there from about 500 A.D. to 1300 A.D., and then they left. Why did they leave? Archaeologists are working to solve this mystery.

ancient dwellings of the Ancestral Pueblo people of Mesa Verde in Colorado

Time of the Basket Makers

Let's look back in time to about the year 500, when the Ancestral Pueblo people settled at Mesa Verde. The word *ancestral* has to do with a person's ancestors—their relatives far back in time. A *pueblo* is a village.

At first, the Ancestral Pueblo people lived on top of the mesa. They dug large pits for houses and built roofs out of branches and mud. They used digging sticks to plant corn, beans, and squash. They also gathered nuts, berries, and cactus plants. The Ancestral Pueblo people made beautiful pots and baskets for cooking and storing food. They also made bows, arrows, and spears for hunting.

Time of the Pueblo Builders

Now, let's move ahead in time to around the year 900 A.D. The Ancestral Pueblo people built dwellings above the ground. At first, their dwellings were made of tree branches and bark covered with adobe (mud and straw). Later on, they built houses from blocks of stone. Their homes had *kivas*—round underground rooms used for gatherings. Each kiva had a large hole at the top with a ladder for entering. The Ancestral Pueblo people traded with people who lived far away. They traded their pots for cotton and spun the cotton into yarn for making clothes. They also tried new ways of farming to save water.

Because kivas were underground, people had to enter them by climbing down a ladder through a hole in the roof.

Time of the Cliff Dwellers

Around the year 1150 A.D., the people moved down off the top of the mesa. They built large stone dwellings, or homes, in the cliffs. The people made painted mugs, bowls, and pots. They also made bracelets of stones, rings of bone, and necklaces of shells. There were many more people than before, so they needed a lot more food. They farmed on top of the mesa. But by 1300 A.D., no one lived at Mesa Verde.

Modern Times

Why did the Ancestral Pueblo people leave Mesa Verde? Did enemies drive them away? Did they run out of food? Did something else happen? They left behind millions of things. In 1906, Mesa Verde became a national park. Archaeologists today study the homes and kivas. They have looked at the pots, baskets, and other things left behind for clues. But the reason that the people left Mesa Verde remains a mystery.

Name: _____

Dictionary

Content Vocabulary

adobe
mud and straw bricks that are
baked in the sun

ancient
from a time long ago

archaeologists
scientists who study people of
long ago by digging up pots,
tools, and other things left
behind

dwellings
places where people live

pueblo
a Native American village
built from stone and adobe

spears
tools used for hunting that
have sharp points and long,
straight handles

Academic Vocabulary

unusual
not common or ordinary

gatherings
meetings

mystery
something that is hidden
or unknown

Write a sentence that includes a vocabulary word.

_____

_____

Identify Information

You can understand a text better if you read it more than once. Look for the following information as you read the article again. Put a check mark in the box after you complete each task.

		I did it!
🖊	Highlight the name of the state where Mesa Verde is located.	☐
—	Draw a line under the sentence that explains how the Basket Makers planted their food.	☐
○	Circle the four words that the author gives definitions for.	☐
★	Draw a star beside the paragraph about the time period when the people built cliff dwellings.	☐
✖	Put an X by the paragraph that tells why the people may have left Mesa Verde.	☐
[ ]	Put brackets around any sentences about the work that archaeologists are doing today at Mesa Verde.	☐
!	Put an exclamation point beside any information that surprised or interested you.	☐
?	Put a question mark beside any words or sentences you don't understand.	☐

Answer Questions

••

Use information from the article to answer each question.

1. The word *mesa* means _____.
   - Ⓐ a relative far back in time
   - Ⓑ the roof of a pit house
   - Ⓒ a way to farm to save water
   - Ⓓ high land that is flat on top

2. Around the year 1150 A.D., the Ancestral Pueblo people _____.
   - Ⓐ left Mesa Verde for good
   - Ⓑ built pueblos in the cliffs
   - Ⓒ made a national park
   - Ⓓ dug large pits for houses

3. The Ancestral Pueblo people _____.
   - Ⓐ grew corn, beans, and squash
   - Ⓑ never hunted
   - Ⓒ did not eat nuts, berries, and cactus
   - Ⓓ grew their own cotton

4. Describe what a kiva is like.

   _____

   _____

5. Make a long list of items the Ancestral Pueblo people made.

   _____

   _____

   _____

Name: _____

Apply Vocabulary

Use a word from the word box to complete each sentence.

Word Box

ancient	mystery	pueblo
adobe	unusual	archaeologists
dwellings	spears	gatherings

1. It is a _____ why the Ancestral Pueblo people left Mesa Verde.

2. _____ have studied the kivas at Mesa Verde.

3. Many people lived in a _____ built into the cliff.

4. Mesa Verde is an ancient place with an _____ history.

5. The earliest _____ of the Ancestral Pueblo people were pits with roofs.

6. The Ancestral Pueblo people held _____ in kivas.

7. _____ was a material used to make dwellings.

8. The Ancestral Pueblo people used _____ for hunting.

9. Archaeologists have studied the _____ kivas.

Name: _____

Time Order

....

A text that has a **time order** structure gives the main idea and gives the details in the order in which they happen.

Authors use these signal words to create a **time order** structure:

Signal Words

at first	now	then	next
later on	in time	when	during

1. What happened at Mesa Verde between the years 500 A.D. and 1300 A.D.?

   _____

2. Write the sentence from the article that tells what part of the mesa the people lived on, at first.

   _____

   _____

3. When did the people stop living on top of the mesa?

   _____

   Write the sentence from the article that tells you so.

   _____

   _____

Name: _____

Write About It

Explain what archaeologists know about how the Ancestral Pueblo people lived. Include details about how archaeologists got their information.

Leaving Home

_____

_____

_____

_____

_____

_____

_____

_____

_____

_____

_____

_____

_____

_____

_____

_____

_____

Social Studies Article
Text Structure: Question and Answer

About Banks

Lesson Objective

Students will write an argument for why it is a good idea for a person to have both a checking account and a savings account.

Content Knowledge

Banks are institutions where people can save money and earn interest, and where they can borrow money and pay interest.

Lesson Preparation

Reproduce and distribute one copy of the article, dictionary page, and activity pages to each student.

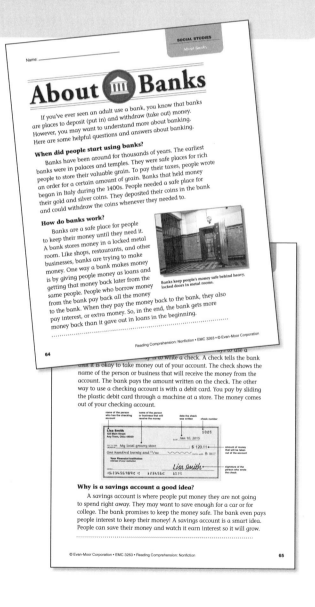

1 Read Aloud the Article

Read aloud *About Banks*. Have students follow along silently as you read.

2 Introduce the Vocabulary

Content Vocabulary

Read aloud the Content Vocabulary words and definitions. Point out that the word *check* has several meanings. It may mean to examine something to see if it is correct. For example, a teacher checks student papers. But in this article, a *check* is a written note giving a bank permission to pay an amount of money from a checking account. Discuss definitions and usage as needed.

Academic Vocabulary

Next, read aloud the Academic Vocabulary words and definitions. Discuss definitions and usage as needed. Then read these context sentences from the article, emphasizing the Academic Vocabulary words:

*They were safe places for wealthy people to store their **valuable** grain.*

*The check shows the name of the person or **business** that will receive the money from the account.*

3 Students Read the Article

Have students read the article independently, with a partner, or in small groups. After students read, guide a discussion about the article. Direct students' attention to graphic elements or visual aids.

4 Identify Information

Explain that students will locate important information in the article. After students complete the activity, allow time for a question-and-answer session.

5 Answer Questions

Encourage students to use the article to answer the questions and/or check their answers.

6 Apply Vocabulary

Have students reread the article before they complete the vocabulary activity. Optional: Have students mark each vocabulary word as they read.

7 Examine Text Structure

Read aloud the Question and Answer description and Signal Words. Then have students read the article again, underlining signal words in red. Then guide students in completing the activity.

8 Write About It:
Having Bank Accounts

Have students complete the writing activity independently or in small groups.

About 🏛 Banks

If you've ever seen an adult use a bank, you know that banks are places to deposit (put in) and withdraw (take out) money. However, you may want to understand more about banking. Here are some helpful questions and answers about banking.

When did people start using banks?

Banks have been around for thousands of years. The earliest banks were in palaces and temples. They were safe places for rich people to store their valuable grain. To pay their taxes, people wrote an order for a certain amount of grain. Banks that held money began in Italy during the 1400s. People needed a safe place for their gold and silver coins. They deposited their coins in the bank and could withdraw the coins whenever they needed to.

How do banks work?

Banks are a safe place for people to keep their money until they need it. A bank stores money in a locked metal room. Like shops, restaurants, and other businesses, banks are trying to make money. One way a bank makes money is by giving people money as loans and getting that money back later from the same people. People who borrow money from the bank pay back all the money

Banks keep people's money safe behind heavy, locked doors in metal rooms.

to the bank. When they pay the money back to the bank, they also pay interest, or extra money. So, in the end, the bank gets more money back than it gave out in loans in the beginning.

What is a bank account?

A bank account is a record, or list, of the money that a person deposits in a bank. The bank and the person both keep track of how much money goes into and comes out of the account. The two main kinds of accounts are a checking account and a savings account.

How does a checking account work?

A checking account is used to pay for things. You can use it instead of carrying a lot of money with you. There are two ways to use a checking account. One way is to write a check. A check tells the bank that it is okay to take money out of your account. The check shows the name of the person or business that will receive the money from the account. The bank pays the amount written on the check. The other way to use a checking account is with a debit card. You pay by sliding the plastic debit card through a machine at a store. The money comes out of your checking account.

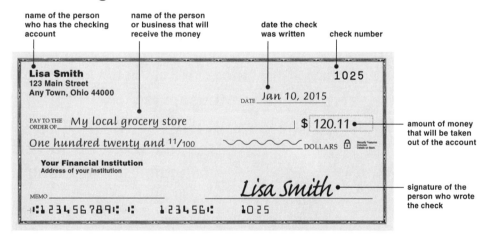

Why is a savings account a good idea?

A savings account is where people put money they are not going to spend right away. They may want to save enough for a car or for college. The bank promises to keep the money safe. The bank even pays people interest to keep their money! A savings account is a smart idea. People can save their money and watch it earn interest so it will grow.

Dictionary

Content Vocabulary

account
a record of the money that a person keeps in a bank

check
a written order telling a bank to pay an amount from a person's checking account

debit card
a small plastic card used to buy things; the money comes out of a checking account

deposit
to put money into an account

loans
money that is lent to people to use for a period of time

temples
buildings where some people go to practice their religion

withdraw
to take money out of an account

Academic Vocabulary

valuable
having worth or value

business
a place where people work to make money and where customers spend money

Write a sentence that includes a vocabulary word.

_____

_____

Name: _____

Identify Information

You can understand a text better if you read it more than once. Look for the following information as you read the article again. Put a check mark in the box after you complete each task.

		I did it!
⭕	Circle the word for putting money into an account.	☐
☐	Draw a box around the word for taking money out of an account.	☐
—	Draw a line under the sentence that tells what types of buildings the earliest banks were located in.	☐
★	Draw a star beside the paragraph that tells how banks make money.	☐
✖	Put an X next to the sentence that names the two main kinds of bank accounts.	☐
🖊	Highlight the sentence that tells what a checking account is used for.	☐
[ ]	Put brackets around the sentence that explains what a savings account is.	☐
!	Put an exclamation point beside any information that surprised or interested you.	☐
?	Put a question mark beside any words or sentences you don't understand.	☐

Answer Questions

Use information from the article to answer each question.

1. The earliest banks held _____.

   Ⓐ checks

   Ⓑ gold and silver coins

   Ⓒ plastic cards

   Ⓓ valuable grain

2. Banks make money by _____.

   Ⓐ collecting interest from people

   Ⓑ printing money

   Ⓒ selling cars

   Ⓓ keeping grain in metal rooms

3. When a person writes a check, he or she writes _____.

   Ⓐ the name of the bank owner

   Ⓑ the amount of money that should be paid

   Ⓒ a letter to the bank

   Ⓓ nothing

4. Name two kinds of bank accounts.

   a. _____

   b. _____

5. Why is a checking account useful?

   _____

   _____

Apply Vocabulary

Use a word from the word box to complete each sentence.

Word Box		
withdraw	account	check
debit card	valuable	deposit
business	temples	loans

1. People who get bank _____ must pay back the money.

2. If you _____ money in a savings account, the total grows.

3. A bank is a safe place for people's _____ money.

4. To save for a vacation, you can put some money in a savings

   _____ each week.

5. When you _____ money from a bank, you take it out.

6. If you buy food at a store, you can pay with a _____ or a debit card.

7. A _____ is made of plastic.

8. A bank, like a restaurant, is a place of _____.

9. _____ are religious places that held the first banks.

Question and Answer

··

> A text that has a **question-and-answer** structure asks questions
> and gives answers to those questions.

Authors use these signal words to create a **question-and-answer**
structure:

Signal Words

who	where	why
what	when	how

1. What is the first question in bold print in the article?

   _____

   Write the answer to this question in your own words.

   _____

2. Which question begins with the signal word *why*?

   _____

   Write the answer to this question in your own words.

   _____

   _____

3. Write the two questions from the article that use the signal word *how.*

   a. _____

   b. _____

Name: _____

Write About It

Write an argument for why it's a good idea to have both a checking account and a savings account. Include facts and details from the article.

Having Bank Accounts

_____

_____

_____

_____

_____

_____

_____

_____

_____

_____

_____

_____

_____

_____

_____

_____

_____

_____

_____

The Great Lakes

Lesson Objective   Students will explain how the Great Lakes were created and how they helped cause cities and farms to grow.

Content Knowledge   Glacial movement and melt formed the Great Lakes long ago. In more recent history, the Great Lakes provided easy transportation for settlers.

Lesson Preparation

Reproduce and distribute one copy of the article, dictionary page, and activity pages to each student.

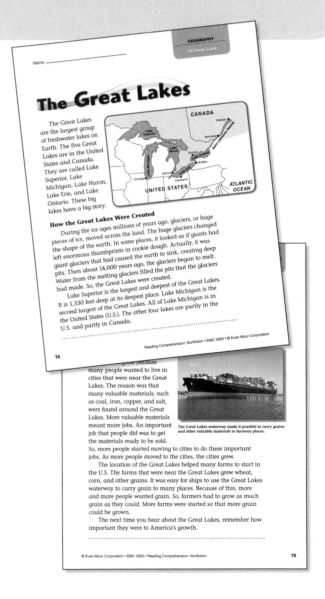

GEOGRAPHY
The Great Lakes

Name:

The Great Lakes

The Great Lakes are the largest group of freshwater lakes on Earth. The five Great Lakes are in the United States and Canada. They are called Lake Superior, Lake Michigan, Lake Huron, Lake Erie, and Lake Ontario. These big lakes have a big story.

How the Great Lakes Were Created

During the ice ages millions of years ago, glaciers, or huge pieces of ice, moved across the land. The huge glaciers changed the shape of the earth. In some places, it looked as if giants had left enormous thumbprints in cookie dough. Actually, it was giant glaciers that had caused the earth to sink, creating deep pits. Then about 14,000 years ago, the glaciers began to melt. Water from the melting glaciers filled the pits that the glaciers had made. So, the Great Lakes were created.

Lake Superior is the largest and deepest of the Great Lakes. It is 1,330 feet deep at its deepest place. Lake Michigan is the second largest of the Great Lakes. All of Lake Michigan is in the United States (U.S.). The other four lakes are partly in the U.S. and partly in Canada.

Reading Comprehension: Nonfiction • EMC 3263 • © Evan-Moor Corporation

74

... grow because many people wanted to live in cities that were near the Great Lakes. The reason was that many valuable materials, such as coal, iron, copper, and salt, were found around the Great Lakes. More valuable materials meant more jobs. An important job that people did was to get the materials ready to be sold.

The Great Lakes waterway made it possible to carry grains and other valuable materials to faraway places.

So, more people started moving to cities to do these important jobs. As more people moved to the cities, the cities grew.

The location of the Great Lakes helped many farms to start in the U.S. The farms that were near the Great Lakes grew wheat, corn, and other grains. It was easy for ships to use the Great Lakes waterway to carry grain to many places. Because of this, more and more people wanted grain. So, farmers had to grow as much grain as they could. More farms were started so that more grain could be grown.

The next time you hear about the Great Lakes, remember how important they were to America's growth.

© Evan-Moor Corporation • EMC 3263 • Reading Comprehension: Nonfiction   75

1   Read Aloud the Article

Read aloud *The Great Lakes*. Have students follow along silently as you read.

2   Introduce the Vocabulary

Content Vocabulary

Read aloud the Content Vocabulary words and definitions. Point out that two of the words come from the French language. *Canal* comes from the French word for channel, a body of water. *Glacier* comes from the French word for ice. Discuss definitions and usage as needed.

Academic Vocabulary

Next, read aloud the Academic Vocabulary words and definitions. Discuss definitions and usage as needed. Then read these context sentences from the article, emphasizing the Academic Vocabulary words:

*The Great Lakes are **connected** by rivers and canals.*

*The reason was that many valuable **materials**, such as coal, iron, copper, and salt, were found around the Great Lakes.*

3   Students Read the Article

Have students read the article independently, with a partner, or in small groups. After students read, guide a discussion about the article. Direct students' attention to graphic elements or visual aids.

4   Identify Information

Explain that students will locate important information in the article. After students complete the activity, allow time for a question-and-answer session.

5   Answer Questions

Encourage students to use the article to answer the questions and/or check their answers.

6   Apply Vocabulary

Have students reread the article before they complete the vocabulary activity. Optional: Have students mark each vocabulary word as they read.

7   Examine Text Structure

Read aloud the Cause and Effect description and Signal Words. Then have students read the article again, underlining signal words in red. Then guide students in completing the activity.

8   Write About It:
An Important Waterway

Have students complete the writing activity independently or in small groups.

Name: _____

The Great Lakes

The Great Lakes are the largest group of freshwater lakes on Earth. The five Great Lakes are in the United States and Canada. They are called Lake Superior, Lake Michigan, Lake Huron, Lake Erie, and Lake Ontario. These big lakes have a big story.

How the Great Lakes Were Created

During the ice ages millions of years ago, glaciers, or huge pieces of ice, moved across the land. The huge glaciers changed the shape of the earth. In some places, it looked as if giants had left enormous thumbprints in cookie dough. Actually, it was giant glaciers that had caused the earth to sink, creating deep pits. Then about 14,000 years ago, the glaciers began to melt. Water from the melting glaciers filled the pits that the glaciers had made. So, the Great Lakes were created.

Lake Superior is the largest and deepest of the Great Lakes. It is 1,330 feet deep at its deepest place. Lake Michigan is the second largest of the Great Lakes. All of Lake Michigan is in the United States (U.S.). The other four lakes are partly in the U.S. and partly in Canada.

A Waterway

The Great Lakes are connected by rivers and canals. Together, the lakes, rivers, and canals make up the Great Lakes waterway. In America's early days, many people found it helpful that the Great Lakes waterway existed.

The Lakes Were Important for Growing Cities and Farms

The Great Lakes helped cities and farms grow. They helped cities grow because many people wanted to live in cities that were near the Great Lakes. The reason was that many valuable materials, such as coal, iron, copper, and salt, were found around the Great Lakes. More valuable materials meant more jobs. An important job that people did was to get the materials ready to be sold.

The Great Lakes waterway made it possible to carry grains and other valuable materials to faraway places.

So, more people started moving to cities to do these important jobs. As more people moved to the cities, the cities grew.

The location of the Great Lakes helped many farms to start in the U.S. The farms that were near the Great Lakes grew wheat, corn, and other grains. It was easy for ships to use the Great Lakes waterway to carry grain to many places. Because of this, more and more people wanted grain. So, farmers had to grow as much grain as they could. More farms were started so that more grain could be grown.

The next time you hear about the Great Lakes, remember how important they were to America's growth.

Dictionary

Content Vocabulary

canals
waterways dug across land for
ships to go through

glaciers
very large pieces of ice

ice ages
times long ago when ice
covered the world

iron
a valuable type of metal

waterway
a body of water that ships
can travel through

Academic Vocabulary

connected
joined together

materials
things used to make other
things

Write a sentence that includes a vocabulary word.

_____

_____

Name: _____

Identify Information

You can understand a text better if you read it more than once. Look for the following information as you read the article again. Put a check mark in the box after you complete each task.

		I did it!
[ ]	Put brackets around the sentence that names all five Great Lakes.	☐
◯	Circle the sentence that explains what glaciers are.	☐
⬟	Highlight the sentence that tells which of the Great Lakes is the largest and deepest.	☐
—	Draw a line under the sentence that tells what connects all of the Great Lakes.	☐
★	Draw a star beside the paragraph that tells about the growth of cities.	☐
✖	Put an X next to the paragraph that tells about the growth of farms.	☐
!	Put an exclamation point beside any information that surprised or interested you.	☐
?	Put a question mark beside any words or sentences you don't understand.	☐

Answer Questions

Use information from the article to answer each question.

1. The two largest Great Lakes are _____.
   - Ⓐ Superior and Huron
   - Ⓑ Michigan and Ontario
   - Ⓒ Superior and Michigan
   - Ⓓ Erie and Huron

2. The Great Lakes were created because glaciers _____.
   - Ⓐ created large areas of farmland
   - Ⓑ caused the earth to rise into mountains
   - Ⓒ made the earth sink and get full of water
   - Ⓓ made one giant lake on the earth

3. Lake _____ is the only Great Lake that is completely in the United States.
   - Ⓐ Michigan
   - Ⓑ Huron
   - Ⓒ Ontario
   - Ⓓ Superior

4. What led to the growth of cities around the Great Lakes?

   _____

   _____

5. Why did more and more farms grow around the Great Lakes?

   _____

   _____

Name: _____

Apply Vocabulary

Use a word from the word box to complete each sentence.

Word Box

| glaciers | waterway | materials | iron |
| ice ages | connected | canals | |

1. The Great Lakes _____ includes rivers, canals, and the Great Lakes.

2. Some car parts are made of _____, a type of metal.

3. About 14,000 years ago, the _____ began to melt.

4. Because the Great Lakes are _____, water can flow from one lake to another.

5. Certain _____ are used to make steel.

6. _____ are man-made waterways for ships to travel through.

7. The _____ were times when glaciers shaped the earth.

Cause and Effect

A text that has a **cause-and-effect** structure describes a cause and tells about the result of it.

Authors use these signal words to create a **cause-and-effect** structure:

Signal Words

created	because of
effects of	for this reason

1. What caused the Great Lakes to fill up?

   _____

   _____

2. Write the sentence that tells what changed the shape of the earth.

   _____

3. Write the sentence that tells what more valuable materials meant.

   _____

   _____

4. Write the sentence that explains why more farms were started.

   _____

   _____

Write About It

Explain how the Great Lakes were created and how they helped cause cities and farms to grow. Include facts and details from the article.

An Important Waterway

_____

_____

_____

_____

_____

_____

_____

_____

_____

_____

_____

_____

_____

_____

Biography Article
Text Structure: Time Order

Sandra Day O'Connor

Lesson Objective	Students will explain who Sandra Day O'Connor is and what she has done during her life.
Content Knowledge	Sandra Day O'Connor was the first woman to serve as a justice on the Supreme Court.

Lesson Preparation

Reproduce and distribute one copy of the article, dictionary page, and activity pages to each student.

BIOGRAPHY
Sandra Day O'Connor

Name: _____

Sandra Day O'Connor

The Lazy B Ranch was wide-open land. It spread across the border between Arizona and New Mexico. It had a little adobe ranch house. In the spring of 1930, Ada Mae Day brought her first baby home to the ranch. The baby's name was Sandra. The baby's father, Harry Day, was the ranch owner. He was there to welcome them home.

Even the cowboys were happy to have a baby around. They made sure there was always wood for the woodstove. They carried water from the well so Mrs. Day could wash baby clothes. They were good babysitters, too. They gave Sandra lots of attention. When she learned to sit up, a cowboy gave her "horsey rides." He held her on his saddle and rode his horse around the yard.

When Sandra was seven, her father gave her a small saddle. Sandra liked being a cowgirl. She loved to ride out with her father when he was working. Sometimes he would climb up a windmill to oil it. (The windmills pumped water from wells deep under the dry earth.) Other times, he checked the water tanks that held rainwater for the animals. He would make sure the animals were healthy and well taken care of. After a big rain, he might pull cows out of the mud with a rope.

As a child, Sandra loved to ride horses. She even had her own saddle.

84

Reading Comprehension: Nonfiction • EMC 3263 • © Evan-Moor Corporation

...ed in 1952.
After law school, Sandra could not find a job. People did not hire women as lawyers in the 1950s. At last, she found a job in California, but it was without pay. People soon saw that she was a good lawyer. She was such a great lawyer that, in the following years, she was paid to work as a lawyer. She also worked as a lawmaker and a judge in Arizona.

Then in 1981, President Reagan chose Sandra Day O'Connor to be a justice on the Supreme Court. The Supreme Court is the highest court in the United States. The Court decides if laws are fair. The Court is made up of nine justices. Before Justice O'Connor, all the justices had been men. The little cowgirl from the Lazy B Ranch grew up to be the first woman justice on the Supreme Court.

Justice Sandra Day O'Connor

© Evan-Moor Corporation • EMC 3263 • Reading Comprehension: Nonfiction

85

1 Read Aloud the Article

Read aloud *Sandra Day O'Connor*. Have students follow along silently as you read.

2 Introduce the Vocabulary

Content Vocabulary
Read aloud the Content Vocabulary words and definitions. Point out that *court* is a multiple-meaning word, or homonym. It can mean a group of judges or the place where they meet. It can also mean a place where certain sports, such as tennis, are played. Explain that *justice* is also a homonym. It can mean a person who is a judge, or it can mean fair treatment. Discuss definitions and usage as needed.

Academic Vocabulary
Next, read aloud the Academic Vocabulary words and definitions. Discuss definitions and usage as needed. Then read these context sentences from the article, emphasizing the Academic Vocabulary words:

*People did not **hire** women as lawyers in the 1950s.*

*At last, she found a job in California, but it was without **pay**.*

3 Students Read the Article

Have students read the article independently, with a partner, or in small groups. After students read, guide a discussion about the article. Direct students' attention to graphic elements or visual aids.

4 Identify Information

Explain that students will locate important information in the article. After students complete the activity, allow time for a question-and-answer session.

5 Answer Questions

Encourage students to use the article to help them answer the questions and/or check their answers.

6 Apply Vocabulary

Have students reread the article before they complete the vocabulary activity. Optional: Have students mark each vocabulary word as they read.

7 Examine Text Structure

Read aloud the Time Order description and Signal Words. Have students read the article again, underlining signal words in red. Then guide students in completing the activity.

8 Write About It:
Growing Up on a Ranch

Have students complete the writing activity independently or in small groups.

Name: _____

Sandra Day O'Connor

The Lazy B Ranch was wide-open land. It spread across the border between Arizona and New Mexico. It had a little adobe ranch house. In the spring of 1930, Ada Mae Day brought her first baby home to the ranch. The baby's name was Sandra. The baby's father, Harry Day, was the ranch owner. He was there to welcome them home.

Even the cowboys were happy to have a baby around. They made sure there was always wood for the woodstove. They carried water from the well so Mrs. Day could wash baby clothes. They were good babysitters, too. They gave Sandra lots of attention. When she learned to sit up, a cowboy gave her "horsey rides." He held her on his saddle and rode his horse around the yard.

As a child, Sandra loved to ride horses. She even had her own saddle.

When Sandra was seven, her father gave her a small saddle. Sandra liked being a cowgirl. She loved to ride out with her father when he was working. Sometimes he would climb up a windmill to oil it. (The windmills pumped water from wells deep under the dry earth.) Other times, he checked the water tanks that held rainwater for the animals. He would make sure the animals were healthy and well taken care of. After a big rain, he might pull cows out of the mud with a rope.

When Sandra was old enough, her parents sent her away to a good school. She lived with her grandmother during those years. Sandra had many friends at school, but she missed her parents and the ranch. She looked forward to summers at home. In 1946, Sandra turned sixteen and started college. She went to Stanford University in California. After college, she went to law school, which is where people study laws. She met another law student named John O'Connor. They were married in 1952.

After law school, Sandra could not find a job. People did not hire women as lawyers in the 1950s. At last, she found a job in California, but it was without pay. People soon saw that she was a good lawyer. She was such a great lawyer that, in the following years, she was paid to work as a lawyer. She also worked as a lawmaker and a judge in Arizona.

Justice Sandra Day O'Connor

Then in 1981, President Reagan chose Sandra Day O'Connor to be a justice on the Supreme Court. The Supreme Court is the highest court in the United States. The Court decides if laws are fair. The Court is made up of nine justices. Before Justice O'Connor, all the justices had been men. The little cowgirl from the Lazy B Ranch grew up to be the first woman justice on the Supreme Court.

Dictionary

Content Vocabulary

adobe
mud and straw bricks that are
baked in the sun

court
a group of judges who meet
to decide cases of the law; the
place where cases of the law
are decided

justice
a judge; a person who decides
cases in a court of law

law school
a school where people study
laws

lawyer
a person who knows the laws
and helps people in court

saddle
a seat for a rider on a horse

windmill
a tall machine with blades that
spin in the wind to pump water

Academic Vocabulary

hire
to give a job to

pay
money you get for doing a job

Write a sentence that includes a vocabulary word.

_____

_____

Name: _____

Identify Information

You can understand a text better if you read it more than once. Look for the following information as you read the article again. Put a check mark in the box after you complete each task.

		I did it!
○	Circle the U.S. states where the Lazy B Ranch was located.	☐
✖	Put an X next to the paragraph that tells how people on the ranch helped take care of the baby.	☐
—	Draw a line under the sentence that explains why windmills were important on the ranch.	☐
★	Draw a star next to the paragraph that tells about the schools Sandra went to.	☐
[ ]	Put brackets around the sentence that tells what people did not do in the 1950s.	☐
🖍	Highlight the sentence that tells what Sandra Day O'Connor was the first to do.	☐
!	Put an exclamation point beside any information that surprised or interested you.	☐
?	Put a question mark beside any words or sentences you don't understand.	☐

Answer Questions

Use information from the article to answer each question.

1. As a child, Sandra Day O'Connor _____.
   - Ⓐ didn't have any friends
   - Ⓑ wanted to be on the Supreme Court
   - Ⓒ was afraid of horses
   - Ⓓ lived in an adobe ranch house

2. As a 16-year-old, Sandra _____.
   - Ⓐ went to Stanford University
   - Ⓑ learned to ride a horse
   - Ⓒ met President Reagan
   - Ⓓ became a cowgirl

3. After law school, Sandra _____.
   - Ⓐ got a job working on a ranch
   - Ⓑ learned that people did not hire women as lawyers
   - Ⓒ missed her parents and the ranch
   - Ⓓ felt ashamed that she had grown up on a ranch

4. How did they get water on the Lazy B Ranch?

   _____

   _____

5. What does the Supreme Court decide?

   _____

Name: _____

Apply Vocabulary

Use a word from the word box to complete each sentence.

Word Box

lawyer	adobe	law school
court	pay	windmill
hire	justice	saddle

1. Sandra was the first woman on the highest _____ in the United States.

2. Sandra went to _____ after she finished college.

3. The first house that Sandra lived in was made of _____.

4. At law school, Sandra studied to become a _____.

5. Sandra was willing to work as a lawyer without _____.

6. As a _____, Sandra helped decide cases in court.

7. Finally, someone in California did _____ Sandra as a lawyer.

8. A _____ pumps water from deep below dry earth.

9. People sit on a _____ when they ride a horse.

Time Order

A text that has a **time order** structure gives the main idea and gives the details in the order in which they happen.

Authors use these signal words to create a **time order** structure:

Signal Words

in the spring	when	at last	before
then	after	following	soon

1. What happened in the spring of 1930?

   _____

2. Write the sentence that tells what President Reagan chose Sandra to do.

   _____

   _____

3. Write two sentences from the article that use **time order** signal words.

   a. _____

   _____

   b. _____

   _____

Write About It

Explain who Sandra Day O'Connor is. Explain what she has done during her life. Include facts and details from the article.

Growing Up on a Ranch

_____

_____

_____

_____

_____

_____

_____

_____

_____

_____

_____

_____

_____

_____

_____

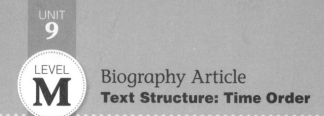

Biography Article
Text Structure: Time Order

Barack Obama

Lesson Objective   Students will write and support an opinion about why Barack Obama has tried to help people who were treated as if they didn't belong.

Content Knowledge   Barack Obama was the first African American to be elected president of the United States.

Lesson Preparation

Reproduce and distribute one copy of the article, dictionary page, and activity pages to each student.

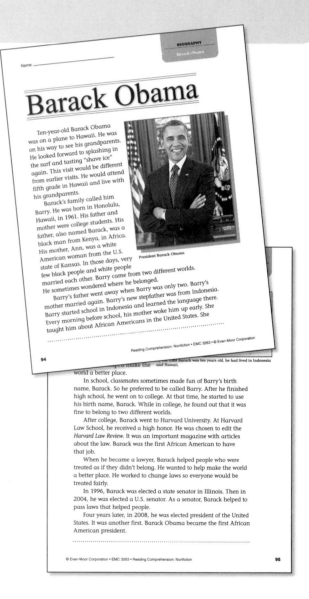

Barack Obama

Ten-year-old Barack Obama was on a plane to Hawaii. He was on his way to see his grandparents. He looked forward to splashing in the surf and tasting "shave ice" again. This visit would be different from earlier visits. He would attend fifth grade in Hawaii and live with his grandparents.

Barack's family called him Barry. He was born in Honolulu, Hawaii, in 1961. His father and mother were college students. His father, also named Barack, was a black man from Kenya, in Africa. His mother, Ann, was a white American woman from the U.S. state of Kansas. In those days, very few black people and white people married each other. Barry came from two different worlds.

Barack's father went away when Barry was only two. Barry's mother married again. Barry's new stepfather was from Indonesia. Barry started school in Indonesia and learned the language there. Every morning before school, his mother woke him up early. She taught him about African Americans in the United States. She

President Barack Obama

Reading Comprehension: Nonfiction • EMC 3263 • © Evan-Moor Corporation

94

...ped make the   and Barack was ten years old, he had lived in Indonesia world a better place.   and Hawaii.

In school, classmates sometimes made fun of Barry's birth name, Barack. So he preferred to be called Barry. After he finished high school, he went on to college. At that time, he started to use his birth name, Barack. While in college, he found out that it was fine to belong to two different worlds.

After college, Barack went to Harvard University. At Harvard Law School, he received a high honor. He was chosen to edit the *Harvard Law Review*. It was an important magazine with articles about the law. Barack was the first African American to have that job.

When he became a lawyer, Barack helped people who were treated as if they didn't belong. He wanted to help make the world a better place. He worked to change laws so everyone would be treated fairly.

In 1996, Barack was elected a state senator in Illinois. Then in 2004, he was elected a U.S. senator. As a senator, Barack helped to pass laws that helped people.

Four years later, in 2008, he was elected president of the United States. It was another first. Barack Obama became the first African American president.

© Evan-Moor Corporation • EMC 3263 • Reading Comprehension: Nonfiction   95

1 Read Aloud the Article

Read aloud *Barack Obama.* Have students follow along silently as you read.

2 Introduce the Vocabulary

Content Vocabulary

Read aloud the Content Vocabulary words and definitions. Point out that *enslaved* has the prefix *en-*. Explain that when this prefix is used, it means that something is happening to a person or a person is doing something. Use the word *enjoy. Joy* is a noun, but when you add *en-*, it becomes a verb. Point out that *surf* is a multiple-meaning word. As a noun, it means waves. As a verb, it means to ride on a surfboard. Discuss definitions and usage as needed.

Academic Vocabulary

Next, read aloud the Academic Vocabulary words and definitions. Discuss definitions and usage as needed. Then read these context sentences from the article, emphasizing the Academic Vocabulary words:

*He would **attend** fifth grade in Hawaii and live with his grandparents.*

*Barry's new **stepfather** was from Indonesia.*

*At Harvard Law School, he received a high **honor**.*

*He was chosen to **edit** the Harvard Law Review.*

3 Students Read the Article

Have students read the article independently, with a partner, or in small groups. After students read, guide a discussion about the article. Direct students' attention to graphic elements or visual aids.

4 Identify Information

Explain that students will locate important information in the article. After students complete the activity, allow time for a question-and-answer session.

5 Answer Questions

Encourage students to use the article to answer the questions and/or check their answers.

6 Apply Vocabulary

Have students reread the article before they complete the vocabulary activity. Optional: Have students mark each vocabulary word as they read.

7 Examine Text Structure

Read aloud the Time Order description and Signal Words. Then have students read the article again, underlining signal words in red. Then guide students in completing the activity.

8 Write About It:
Many Worlds

Have students complete the writing activity independently or in small groups.

Barack Obama

Ten-year-old Barack Obama was on a plane to Hawaii. He was on his way to see his grandparents. He looked forward to splashing in the surf and tasting "shave ice" again. This visit would be different from earlier visits. He would attend fifth grade in Hawaii and live with his grandparents.

Barack's family called him Barry. He was born in Honolulu, Hawaii, in 1961. His father and mother were college students. His father, also named Barack, was a black man from Kenya, in Africa. His mother, Ann, was a white American woman from the U.S. state of Kansas. In those days, very few black people and white people

President Barack Obama

married each other. Barry came from two different worlds. He sometimes wondered where he belonged.

Barry's father went away when Barry was only two. Barry's mother married again. Barry's new stepfather was from Indonesia. Barry started school in Indonesia and learned the language there. Every morning before school, his mother woke him up early. She taught him about African Americans in the United States. She wanted Barry to be proud of who he was. He learned that African Americans had been brought to America and were enslaved. He learned that many people were working for equal rights for everyone. Barry's mother also taught him about African American leaders who helped make the world a better place.

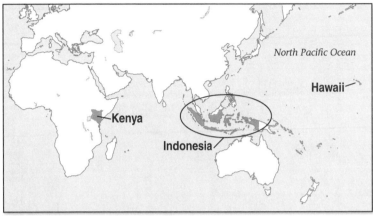

By the time Barack was ten years old, he had lived in Indonesia and Hawaii.

In school, classmates sometimes made fun of Barry's birth name, Barack. So he preferred to be called Barry. After he finished high school, he went on to college. At that time, he started to use his birth name, Barack. While in college, he found out that it was fine to belong to two different worlds.

After college, Barack went to Harvard University. At Harvard Law School, he received a high honor. He was chosen to edit the *Harvard Law Review.* It was an important magazine with articles about the law. Barack was the first African American to have that job.

When he became a lawyer, Barack helped people who were treated as if they didn't belong. He wanted to help make the world a better place. He worked to change laws so everyone would be treated fairly.

In 1996, Barack was elected a state senator in Illinois. Then in 2004, he was elected a U.S. senator. As a senator, Barack helped to pass laws that helped people.

Four years later, in 2008, he was elected president of the United States. It was another first. Barack Obama became the first African American president.

Name: _____

Dictionary

Content Vocabulary

elected
chosen by a vote to do a job

enslaved
forced to work for others
without pay

equal rights
freedoms that all people
should have

shave ice
a Hawaiian treat made with
shaved ice and fruit flavors

surf
large waves that roll onto
the seashore

Academic Vocabulary

attend
to go to

stepfather
a man who marries a child's
mother and is not the child's
birth father

honor
a show of respect

edit
to be in charge of a magazine or
other project; to decide what gets
printed in a magazine

Write a sentence that includes a vocabulary word.

_____

_____

Identify Information

You can understand a text better if you read it more than once. Look for the following information as you read the article again. Put a check mark in the box after you complete each task.

		I did it!
✖	Put an X next to the sentence that mentions two fun things about life in Hawaii.	☐
★	Draw stars beside the names of Barry's parents.	☐
—	Draw a line under any sentences that tell what Barry's mother taught him in Indonesia.	☐
◯	Circle the sentence that explains why Barack preferred to be called Barry.	☐
[ ]	Put brackets around the sentence that explains what the *Harvard Law Review* is.	☐
🖊	Highlight two sentences that tell what Barack Obama was the first to do.	☐
!	Put an exclamation point beside any information that surprised or interested you.	☐
?	Put a question mark beside any words or sentences you don't understand.	☐

Answer Questions

Use information from the article to answer each question.

1. As a child, Barry _____.

   Ⓐ lived only in Hawaii

   Ⓑ went to school in Africa

   Ⓒ spoke only English

   Ⓓ lived in Hawaii and Indonesia

2. Barry's father was from _____.

   Ⓐ Hawaii

   Ⓑ Indonesia

   Ⓒ Africa

   Ⓓ Kansas

3. Barry's mother taught him about _____.

   Ⓐ African American leaders

   Ⓑ the language of Indonesia

   Ⓒ life in Kenya

   Ⓓ how to become a lawyer

4. What honor did Barack Obama receive at Harvard University?

   _____

   _____

5. What happened in 2008?

   _____

   _____

Name: _____

Apply Vocabulary

Use a word from the word box to complete each sentence.

Word Box

enslaved	attend	surf
stepfather	elected	honor
equal rights	shave ice	edit

1. Barack flew to Hawaii to _____ school there.

2. Barack Obama was _____ president in 2008.

3. Barry went to Indonesia with his mother and _____.

4. It was an important job to _____ the *Harvard Law Review.*

5. Barry's mother taught him about _____ for everyone.

6. The first African Americans in the U.S. were _____.

7. Barry was excited about tasting _____ again.

8. You can expect to find beautiful _____ at a Hawaiian beach.

9. It is an _____ when you are asked to do a very important job.

Time Order

....

A text that has a **time order** structure gives the main idea and gives the details in the order in which they happen.

Authors use these signal words to create a **time order** structure:

Signal Words

when	later	at that time
then	while	after
before		

1. Write the sentence that tells where and when Barack Obama was born.

   _____

2. Write the sentence from the article that tells what Barry's mother did every morning in Indonesia.

   _____

   _____

3. Write the sentence that tells what Barry found out at college.

   _____

   _____

   _____

Name: _____

Write About It

....

Explain who Barack Obama is. Explain where he is from and what he has done during his life. Include facts and details from the article.

Many Worlds

_____

_____

_____

_____

_____

_____

_____

_____

_____

_____

_____

_____

_____

_____

_____

_____

Technology Article
Text Structure: Cause and Effect

The Zipper

**Lesson
Objective**   Students will explain how the zipper was invented and patented, and how the zipper got its name.

**Content
Knowledge**   The zipper was patented by Whitcomb Judson in 1893.

Lesson Preparation

Reproduce and distribute one copy of the article, dictionary page, and activity pages to each student.

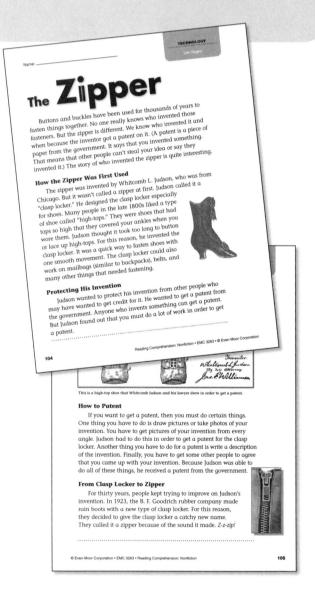

1 Read Aloud the Article

Read aloud *The Zipper.* Have students follow along silently as you read.

2 Introduce the Vocabulary

Content Vocabulary

Read aloud the Content Vocabulary words and definitions. Explain that the word *invented* is the past-tense form of the verb *invent.* Explain that the article also includes two related nouns: *invention* (a new thing that was created) and *inventor* (a person who creates something new). Review with students the suffixes added to make the three words (*-ed, -ion,* and *-or*). Discuss definitions and usage as needed.

Academic Vocabulary

Next, read aloud the Academic Vocabulary words and definitions. Discuss definitions and usage as needed. Then read these context sentences from the article, emphasizing the Academic Vocabulary words:

*Judson wanted to **protect** his invention from other people who may have wanted to get credit for it.*

*You have to get pictures of your invention from every **angle**.*

*Another thing you have to do for a patent is write a **description** of the invention.*

*For thirty years, people kept trying to **improve** on Judson's invention.*

3 Students Read the Article

Have students read the article independently, with a partner, or in small groups. After students read, guide a discussion about the article. Direct students' attention to graphic elements or visual aids.

4 Identify Information

Explain that students will locate important information in the article. After students complete the activity, allow time for a question-and-answer session.

5 Answer Questions

Encourage students to use the article to answer the questions and/or check their answers.

6 Apply Vocabulary

Have students reread the article before they complete the vocabulary activity. Optional: Have students mark each vocabulary word as they read.

7 Examine Text Structure

Read aloud the Cause and Effect description and Signal Words. Then have students read the article again, underlining signal words in red. Then guide students in completing the activity.

8 Write About It:
How the Zipper Was Created

Have students complete the writing activity independently or in small groups.

The Zipper

Buttons and buckles have been used for thousands of years to fasten things together. No one really knows who invented those fasteners. But the zipper is different. We know who invented it and when because the inventor got a patent on it. (A patent is a piece of paper from the government. It says that you invented something. That means that other people can't steal your idea or say they invented it.) The story of who invented the zipper is quite interesting.

How the Zipper Was First Used

The zipper was invented by Whitcomb L. Judson, who was from Chicago. But it wasn't called a zipper at first. Judson called it a "clasp locker." He designed the clasp locker especially for shoes. Many people in the late 1800s liked a type of shoe called "high-tops." They were shoes that had tops so high that they covered your ankles when you wore them. Judson thought it took too long to button or lace up high-tops. For this reason, he invented the clasp locker. It was a quick way to fasten shoes with one smooth movement. The clasp locker could also work on mailbags (similar to backpacks), belts, and many other things that needed fastening.

Protecting His Invention

Judson wanted to protect his invention from other people who may have wanted to get credit for it. He wanted to get a patent from the government. Anyone who invents something can get a patent. But Judson found out that you must do a lot of work in order to get a patent.

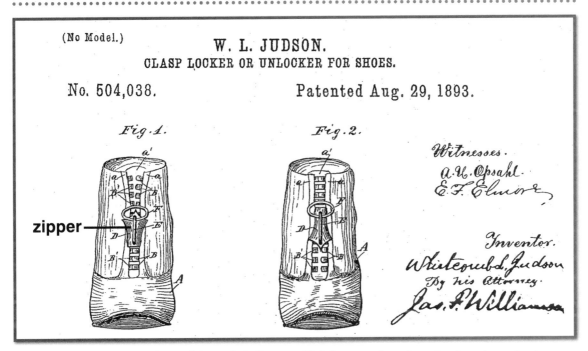

(No Model.)

W. L. JUDSON.
CLASP LOCKER OR UNLOCKER FOR SHOES.

No. 504,038.   Patented Aug. 29, 1893.

Fig. 1.   *Fig. 2.*

Witnesses.
A. U. Opsahl.
E. F. Elmore

Inventor.
Whitcomb L. Judson
By his Attorney.
Jas. F. Williamson

zipper

This is a high-top shoe that Whitcomb Judson and his lawyer drew in order to get a patent.

How to Patent

If you want to get a patent, then you must do certain things. One thing you have to do is draw pictures or take photos of your invention. You have to get pictures of your invention from every angle. Judson had to do this in order to get a patent for the clasp locker. Another thing you have to do for a patent is write a description of the invention. Finally, you have to get some other people to agree that you came up with your invention. Because Judson was able to do all of these things, he received a patent from the government.

From Clasp Locker to Zipper

For thirty years, people kept trying to improve on Judson's invention. In 1923, the B. F. Goodrich rubber company made rain boots with a new type of clasp locker. For this reason, they decided to give the clasp locker a catchy new name. They called it a zipper because of the sound it made. *Z-z-zip!*

Dictionary

Content Vocabulary

clasp
a small hook that holds parts together

fasten
to join two things together

invented
created something new

patent
a piece of paper showing that you own an invention

Academic Vocabulary

protect
to keep safe

angle
a side or a view of something

description
words that tell about something

improve
to make better

Write a sentence that includes a vocabulary word.

_____

_____

Name: _____

Identify Information

You can understand a text better if you read it more than once. Look for the following information as you read the article again. Put a check mark in the box after you complete each task.

		I did it!
✖	Put an X next to the paragraph that explains how we know who invented the zipper.	☐
◯	Circle two words that describe the movement of the clasp locker as it fastened shoes.	☐
🖊	Highlight any sentences that tell what Judson designed the clasp locker for especially.	☐
—	Draw a line under the sentence that tells why Judson wanted to get a patent.	☐
★	Draw a star by the paragraph that describes what you have to do in order to get a patent.	☐
[ ]	Put brackets around the sentence that mentions the year when the clasp locker got its new name.	☐
!	Put an exclamation point beside any information that surprised or interested you.	☐
?	Put a question mark beside any words or sentences you don't understand.	☐

Answer Questions

....

Use information from the article to answer each question.

1. The zipper was invented _____.
   - Ⓐ thousands of years ago
   - Ⓑ at the same time as the buckle
   - Ⓒ by Whitcomb L. Judson in 1893
   - Ⓓ by B. F. Goodrich in 1923

2. The inventor of the zipper wanted to make _____.
   - Ⓐ a new type of rain boot
   - Ⓑ a quick fastener for shoes
   - Ⓒ a new way to draw pictures
   - Ⓓ a new type of mailbag

3. The inventor wrote about the clasp locker _____.
   - Ⓐ in order to get a patent on it
   - Ⓑ in order to tell newspaper readers about it
   - Ⓒ in order to sell it to B. F. Goodrich
   - Ⓓ because he couldn't draw well

4. What do the patent drawings show?

   _____

   _____

5. How did the zipper get its name?

   _____

   _____

Apply Vocabulary

....

Use a word from the word box to complete each sentence.

Word Box			
clasp	invented	fasten	patent
angle	improve	protect	description

1. Each drawing shows the clasp locker from a different

   _____.

2. Judson's _____ locker worked on shoes, belts, mailbags, and many other things.

3. Sometimes, people try to _____ an invention because they think they can make it better.

4. Buttons, buckles, and zippers are used to _____ things.

5. Judson _____ the clasp locker.

6. To get a patent, you must write a _____ of your invention.

7. Judson wanted to get a _____ so he could own the clasp locker invention.

8. A patent is a piece of paper from the government that can

   _____ an invention and its inventor.

Name: _____

Cause and Effect

....

A text that has a **cause-and-effect** structure describes a cause and tells what happened as a result of it.

Authors use these signal words to create a **cause-and-effect** structure:

Signal Words

if . . . then	for this reason
because	in order to

1. How do we know who invented the zipper?

   _____

   _____

2. Write a sentence from the article that uses a **cause-and-effect** signal word.

   _____

   _____

3. What caused Judson to invent the clasp locker?

   _____

   _____

Write About It

Explain how the zipper was invented and patented. Explain how the zipper got its name. Include facts and details from the article.

How the Zipper Was Created

_____

_____

_____

_____

_____

_____

_____

_____

_____

_____

_____

_____

_____

_____

_____

_____

Answer Key

Unit 1

Page 16

Page 18

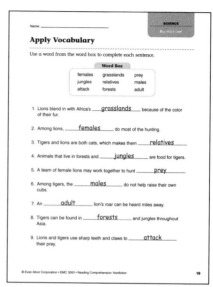

Page 19

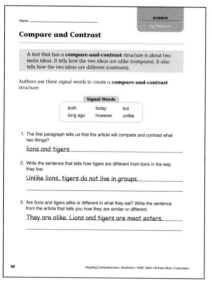

Page 20

Unit 2

Page 26

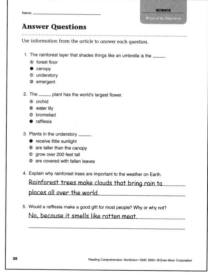

Page 28

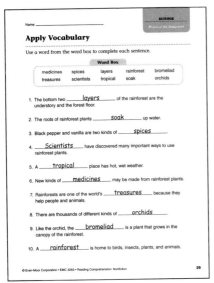

Apply Vocabulary

Use a word from the word box to complete each sentence.

Word Box
medicines spices layers rainforest bromeliad
treasures scientists tropical soak orchids

1. The bottom two __layers__ of the rainforest are the understory and the forest floor.

2. The roots of rainforest plants __soak__ up water.

3. Black pepper and vanilla are two kinds of __spices__.

4. __Scientists__ have discovered many important ways to use rainforest plants.

5. A __tropical__ place has hot, wet weather.

6. New kinds of __medicines__ may be made from rainforest plants.

7. Rainforests are one of the world's __treasures__ because they help people and animals.

8. There are thousands of different kinds of __orchids__.

9. Like the orchid, the __bromeliad__ is a plant that grows in the canopy of the rainforest.

10. A __rainforest__ is home to birds, insects, plants, and animals.

Page 29

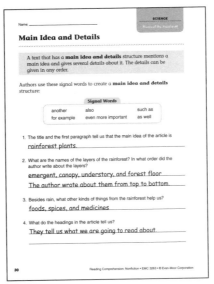

Main Idea and Details

A text that has a **main idea and details** structure mentions a main idea and gives several details about it. The details can be given in any order.

Authors use these signal words to create a **main idea and details** structure:

Signal Words
another also such as
for example even more important as well

1. The title and the first paragraph tell us that the main idea of the article is __rainforest plants.__

2. What are the names of the layers of the rainforest? In what order did the author write about the layers?
__emergent, canopy, understory, and forest floor__
__The author wrote about them from top to bottom.__

3. Besides rain, what other kinds of things from the rainforest help us?
__foods, spices, and medicines__

4. What do the headings in the article tell us?
__They tell us what we are going to read about.__

Page 30

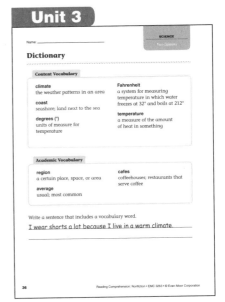

Unit 3

Dictionary

Content Vocabulary

climate
the weather patterns in an area

coast
seashore; land next to the sea

degrees (°)
units of measure for temperature

Fahrenheit
a system for measuring temperature in which water freezes at 32° and boils at 212°

temperature
a measure of the amount of heat in something

Academic Vocabulary

region
a certain place, space, or area

average
usual; most common

cafes
coffeehouses; restaurants that serve coffee

Write a sentence that includes a vocabulary word.
__I wear shorts a lot because I live in a warm climate.__

Page 36

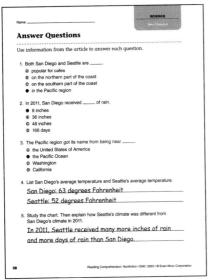

Answer Questions

Use information from the article to answer each question.

1. Both San Diego and Seattle are ___
   Ⓐ popular for cafes
   Ⓑ on the northern part of the coast
   Ⓒ on the southern part of the coast
   ● in the Pacific region

2. In 2011, San Diego received ___ of rain.
   ● 9 inches
   Ⓑ 36 inches
   Ⓒ 48 inches
   Ⓓ 166 days

3. The Pacific region got its name from being near ___
   Ⓐ the United States of America
   ● the Pacific Ocean
   Ⓒ Washington
   Ⓓ California

4. List San Diego's average temperature and Seattle's average temperature.
__San Diego: 63 degrees Fahrenheit__
__Seattle: 52 degrees Fahrenheit__

5. Study the chart. Then explain how Seattle's climate was different from San Diego's climate in 2011.
__In 2011, Seattle received many more inches of rain__
__and more days of rain than San Diego.__

Page 38

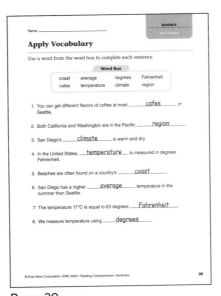

Apply Vocabulary

Use a word from the word box to complete each sentence.

Word Box
coast average degrees Fahrenheit
cafes temperature climate region

1. You can get different flavors of coffee at most __cafes__ in Seattle.

2. Both California and Washington are in the Pacific __region__.

3. San Diego's __climate__ is warm and dry.

4. In the United States, __temperature__ is measured in degrees Fahrenheit.

5. Beaches are often found on a country's __coast__.

6. San Diego has a higher __average__ temperature in the summer than Seattle.

7. The temperature 17°C is equal to 63 degrees __Fahrenheit__.

8. We measure temperature using __degrees__.

Page 39

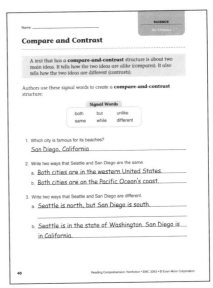

Compare and Contrast

A text that has a **compare-and-contrast** structure is about two main ideas. It tells how the two ideas are alike (compares). It also tells how the two ideas are different (contrasts).

Authors use these signal words to create a **compare-and-contrast** structure:

Signal Words
both but unlike
same while different

1. Which city is famous for its beaches?
__San Diego, California__

2. Write two ways that Seattle and San Diego are the same.
   a. __Both cities are in the western United States.__
   b. __Both cities are on the Pacific Ocean's coast.__

3. Write two ways that Seattle and San Diego are different.
   a. __Seattle is north, but San Diego is south.__

   b. __Seattle is in the state of Washington. San Diego is__
__in California.__

Page 40

Unit 4

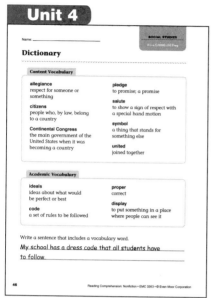

Page 46

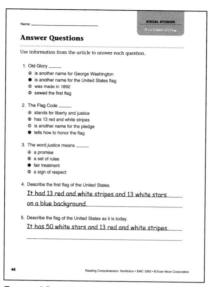

Page 48

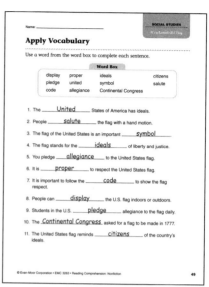

Page 49

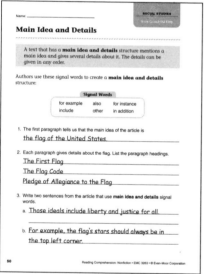

Page 50

Unit 5

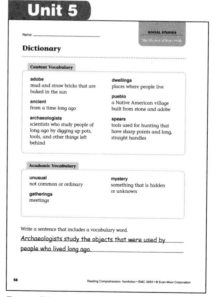

Page 56

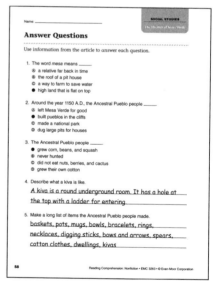

Page 58

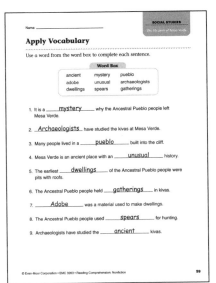

Page 59

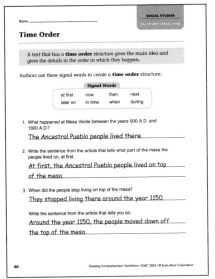

Page 60

Unit 6

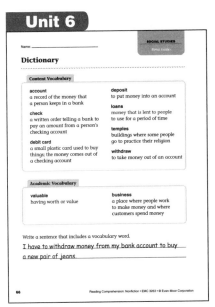

Page 66

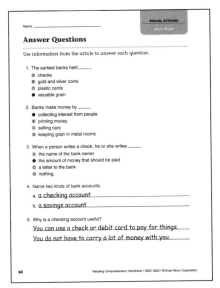

Page 68

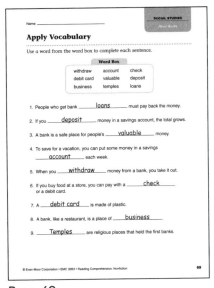

Page 69

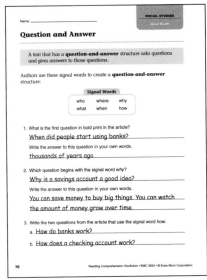

Page 70

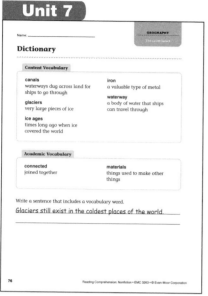

Page 76

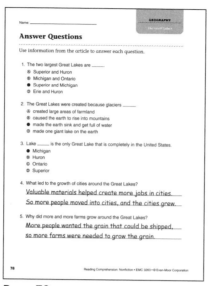

Page 78

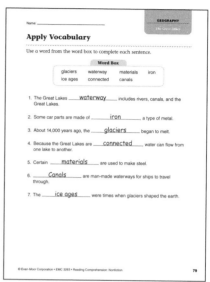

Page 79

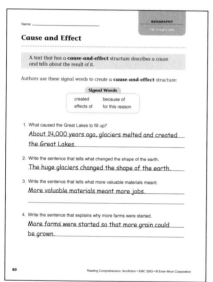

Page 80

Page 86

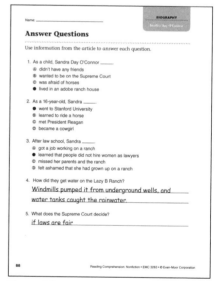

Page 88

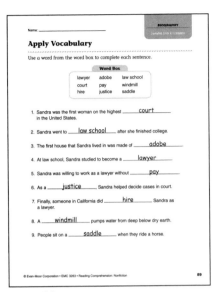

Apply Vocabulary

Use a word from the word box to complete each sentence.

Word Box

lawyer	adobe	law school
court	pay	windmill
hire	justice	saddle

1. Sandra was the first woman on the highest _court_ in the United States.
2. Sandra went to _law school_ after she finished college.
3. The first house that Sandra lived in was made of _adobe_.
4. At law school, Sandra studied to become a _lawyer_.
5. Sandra was willing to work as a lawyer without _pay_.
6. As a _justice_, Sandra helped decide cases in court.
7. Finally, someone in California did _hire_ Sandra as a lawyer.
8. A _windmill_ pumps water from deep below dry earth.
9. People sit on a _saddle_ when they ride a horse.

Page 89

Time Order

A text that has a **time order** structure gives the main idea and gives the details in the order in which they happen.

Authors use these signal words to create a **time order** structure:

Signal Words

| in the spring | when | at last | before |
| then | after | following | soon |

1. What happened in the spring of 1930?
   Sandra Day O'Connor was born.
2. Write the sentence that tells what President Reagan chose Sandra to do.
   Then in 1981, President Reagan chose Sandra Day O'Connor to be a justice on the Supreme Court.
3. Write two sentences from the article that use **time order** signal words.
   a. _After law school, Sandra could not find a job._
   b. _People soon saw that she was a good lawyer._

Page 90

Dictionary

Content Vocabulary

elected
chosen by a vote to do a job

enslaved
forced to work for others without pay

equal rights
freedoms that all people should have

shave ice
a Hawaiian treat made with shaved ice and fruit flavors

surf
large waves that roll onto the seashore

Academic Vocabulary

attend
to go to

stepfather
a man who marries a child's mother and is not the child's birth father

honor
a show of respect

edit
to be in charge of a magazine or other project; to decide what gets printed in a magazine

Write a sentence that includes a vocabulary word.
Megan's parents attend all of her volleyball games.

Page 96

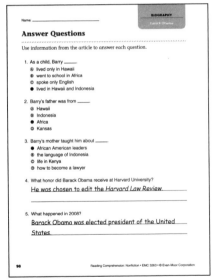

Answer Questions

Use information from the article to answer each question.

1. As a child, Barry _____
   Ⓐ lived only in Hawaii
   Ⓑ went to school in Africa
   Ⓒ spoke only English
   ● lived in Hawaii and Indonesia

2. Barry's father was from _____
   Ⓐ Hawaii
   Ⓑ Indonesia
   ● Africa
   Ⓓ Kansas

3. Barry's mother taught him about _____
   ● African American leaders
   Ⓑ the language of Indonesia
   Ⓒ life in Kenya
   Ⓓ how to become a lawyer

4. What honor did Barack Obama receive at Harvard University?
   He was chosen to edit the Harvard Law Review.

5. What happened in 2008?
   Barack Obama was elected president of the United States.

Page 98

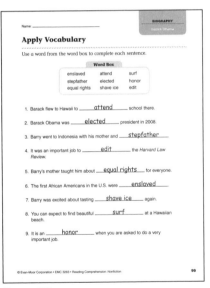

Apply Vocabulary

Use a word from the word box to complete each sentence.

Word Box

enslaved	attend	surf
stepfather	elected	honor
equal rights	shave ice	edit

1. Barack flew to Hawaii to _attend_ school there.
2. Barack Obama was _elected_ president in 2008.
3. Barry went to Indonesia with his mother and _stepfather_.
4. It was an important job to _edit_ the Harvard Law Review.
5. Barry's mother taught him about _equal rights_ for everyone.
6. The first African Americans in the U.S. were _enslaved_.
7. Barry was excited about tasting _shave ice_ again.
8. You can expect to find beautiful _surf_ at a Hawaiian beach.
9. It is an _honor_ when you are asked to do a very important job.

Page 99

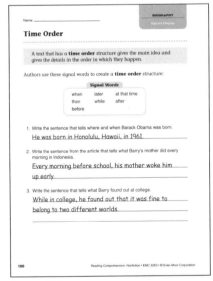

Time Order

A text that has a **time order** structure gives the main idea and gives the details in the order in which they happen.

Authors use these signal words to create a **time order** structure:

Signal Words

when	later	at that time
then	while	after
before		

1. Write the sentence that tells where and when Barack Obama was born.
   He was born in Honolulu, Hawaii, in 1961.
2. Write the sentence from the article that tells what Barry's mother did every morning in Indonesia.
   Every morning before school, his mother woke him up early.
3. Write the sentence that tells what Barry found out at college.
   While in college, he found out that it was fine to belong to two different worlds.

Page 100

Unit 10

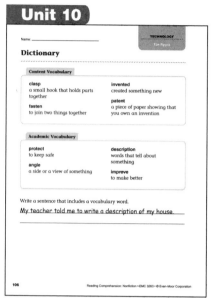

Page 106

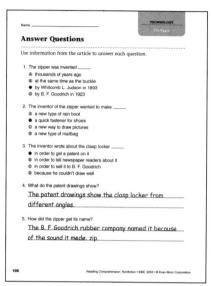

Page 108

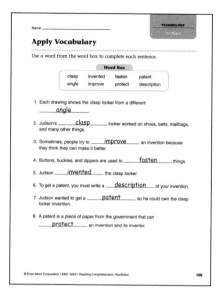

Page 109

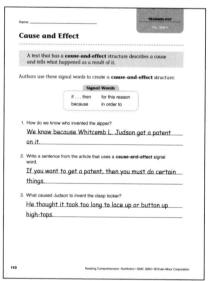

Page 110

Text-Based Writing

Grade 3

SAMPLER

Little Berry, Big Benefit

Lesson Objectives

Writing
Students use information from the health article to write an opinion paragraph.

Vocabulary
Students learn content vocabulary words and use those words to write about blueberries.

Content Knowledge
Students understand that blueberries contain important vitamins and antioxidants.

Essential Understanding
Students understand that people can eat foods such as blueberries to stay healthy and alert.

Prepare

Reproduce and distribute one copy for each student.

1 Unit Focus and Lesson Checklist

Distribute one unit to each student and direct students' attention to the Unit Focus and Lesson Checklist. Tell them they will be able to refer to the focus of the unit as needed while working on the lessons. Instruct students to check off each task on the checklist after they complete it.

Read aloud the focus statements, and verify that students understand their purpose for reading. Ask:

- *What are we going to read about?* (blueberries)

- *What are you going to learn about them?* (how they affect the body)

- *What are you going to write based on this article?* (an opinion paragraph)

2 Learn Vocabulary

Read aloud each content vocabulary word and have students repeat. Then read aloud and discuss the definitions. Point out that the words are related to blueberries and that students will have a better understanding of the words after they read the health article. Have students write the vocabulary words on the provided lines. Then review the Words to Know, and encourage students to ask questions about any words they do not understand.

3 Read the Health Article: *Little Berry, Big Benefit*

Read aloud the health article as students follow along silently. Then have students reread the article independently or in small groups.

4 Answer Questions About the Health Article

To ensure reading comprehension, have students answer the text-dependent questions. Review the answers together.

5 Organize Information

Explain to students that they will use an opinion graphic organizer to help them plan their paragraphs. Guide students in using the text to complete the organizer, rereading the article if needed.

Remind students that an opinion paragraph:

- tells how you feel about something, and
- tells why you feel that way.

6 Write an Opinion Paragraph

Instruct students to complete the writing assignment independently, with a partner, or in small groups.

If needed, review the structure of an opinion paragraph:

- The topic sentence tells your opinion about the subject.
- Details give reasons why you feel that way.

UNIT
13

Little Berry, Big Benefit

Unit Focus

You are going to read a health article about blueberries.

As You Read:

Think about how blueberries affect the human body.

After You Read:

Use information from the article to write an opinion paragraph about blueberries.

Lesson Checklist

Check off each task after you complete it.

☐ **Learn Vocabulary**

☐ **Read the Health Article:**
Little Berry, Big Benefit

☐ **Answer Questions About the**
Health Article

☐ **Organize Information**

☐ **Write an Opinion Paragraph**

Learn Vocabulary

Read the word and its definition.
Then write the vocabulary word on the line.

1. **antioxidants**   things found in or added to food that stop dangerous reactions in your body   _____

2. **contain**   to have within   _____

3. **immune system**   the part of your body that fights infections and keeps you healthy   _____

4. **prevent**   to stop or to keep from happening   _____

5. **sodium**   a mineral found in table salt   _____

Words to Know

blueberry   calories   memory loss   vitamins

Little Berry, Big Benefit

Some foods are better for us than others. Even though blueberries are tiny, they can have a big effect on your body. Blueberries contain important vitamins such as C, A, B-complex, and E. Even a blueberry's color is healthy. The blue comes from antioxidants that are good for you. There are three things blueberries do <u>not</u> have a lot of: fat, sodium, and calories.

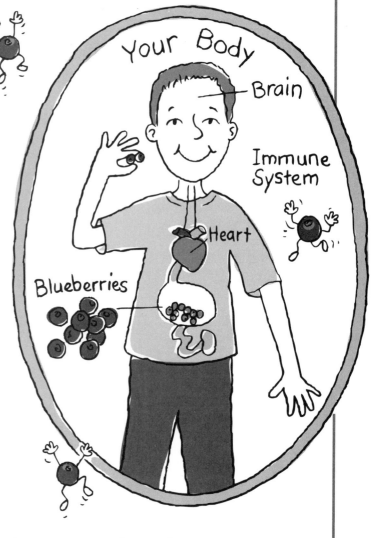

Your brain needs antioxidants to help you stay sharp. Antioxidants can also help prevent your brain from having memory loss when you are much older. Your heart needs antioxidants, too. Your eyes need vitamin A to help you see. Your immune system needs vitamin C and antioxidants to keep you from getting sick. When you have a strong immune system, it's easier for your entire body to stay healthy. Feeling hungry? Eat some blueberries!

Text-Based Writing • EMC 2453 • © Evan-Moor Corporation

Little Berry, Big Benefit

Answer Questions

Read each question. Fill in the circle next to the correct answer.

1. Blueberries contain a lot of ____.

   Ⓐ calories

   Ⓑ vitamins

   Ⓒ fat

2. What gives blueberries their blue color?

   Ⓐ antioxidants

   Ⓑ sodium

   Ⓒ fat

Draw two parts of the body that can be helped by eating blueberries.

UNIT
13

Little Berry, Big Benefit

Organize Information

Read the health article again. Then write information in the graphic organizer that tells your opinion about **why people should or should not eat blueberries**. Support your opinion with reasons.

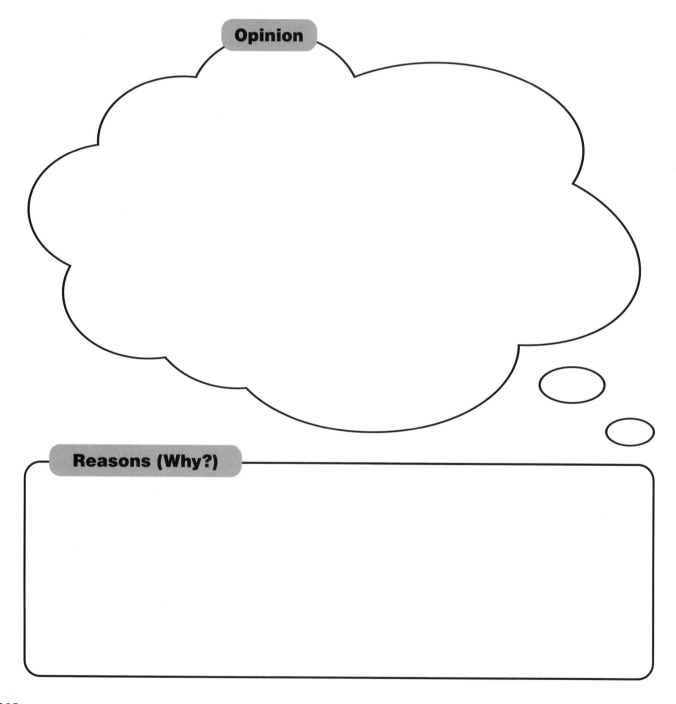

Opinion

Reasons (Why?)

Name _____

Opinion

Write a paragraph that tells your opinion about **blueberries**. Should everyone eat blueberries? Why or why not?

- Use information from your graphic organizer and the health article.

_____
Title

_____

_____

_____

_____

_____

_____

_____

_____

_____

_____